END ZONE

A PHOTOGRAPHIC
CELEBRATION OF FOOTBALL

TEXT BY ANGUS G. GARBER III

·

PHOTOGRAPHS BY JEFFREY E. BLACKMAN

Henry Holt and Company
New York

A FRIEDMAN GROUP BOOK

Copyright © 1987 by Michael Friedman Publishing Group, Inc.

Published in the United States by Henry Holt and Company, Inc.,
521 Fifth Avenue, New York, New York 10175.

Library of Congress Catalog Card Number: 87-45557

ISBN 0-8050-0556-0

First American Edition

END ZONE: A Photographic Celebration of Football was prepared and produced
by Michael Friedman Publishing Group, Inc., 15 West 26th Street,
New York, New York 10010.

Editor: Bruce Lubin
Art Director: Mary Moriarty
Designer: Rod Gonzalez
Photo Editor: Philip Hawthorne
Production Manager: Karen L. Greenberg

Printed in Hong Kong

1 3 5 7 9 10 8 6 4 2

ISBN 0-8050-0556-0

DEDICATION:
To Gerry, who understands

ACKNOWLEDGMENTS:

For those who have shown faith: my parents, Suzanne
and Greg; Greg Stone, the teacher; sports editors Jim
Vincent, Roger Farrell, Rob Tanenbaum, and Jon Pessah;
and my editor Bruce Lubin.

A.G.G. III

INTRODUCTION · 8

CONT

E N T S

Introduction

The name has changed, but the game remains the same. They are modern-day gladiators, these professional football players. Larger than life, they perform in vast gray coliseums seeking the emperor's approval. Yes, the Saints (based now in New Orleans) and the Lions (of Detroit) are still going at it.

Football has been equated with religion and, indeed, in many ways it serves as the opiate of the people, offering escape after a tough week at the office or a release from the bills sitting at home. Leave it at the stadium. It's cheaper than a psychiatrist, and a lot more fun.

And despite what the experts say, football is a beautifully simple game. Forget the off-tackle trap plays, the three-deep zones; the goal is to reach the opponent's end zone and keep him out of yours. Machiavellian rules only apply—push, bully, whack, and connive—just win, baby.

There is a harlequin madness to it all. More than 70,000 people rising and falling, physically and emotionally, in response to a ball thrown from one man to another. Amazing, really, the metaphors at work on a football field. It is good theater, an easy-to-grasp allegory: Good guys, bad guys, pomp and a little circumstance. The bands play, the cheerleaders cheer, and the fans fantasize about winning the big one. The Super Bowl. Has a nice modest ring, doesn't it?

There's nothing subtle about football; that perhaps is its peculiar charm. After all, nothing succeeds like excess.

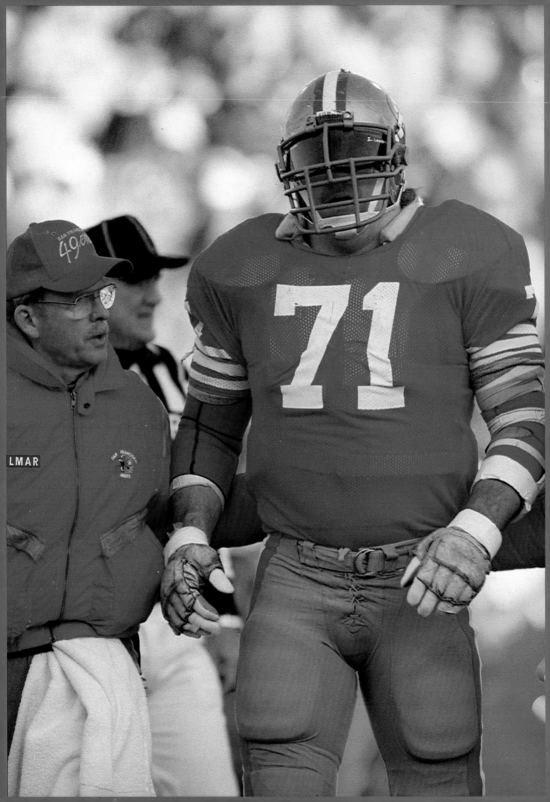

1

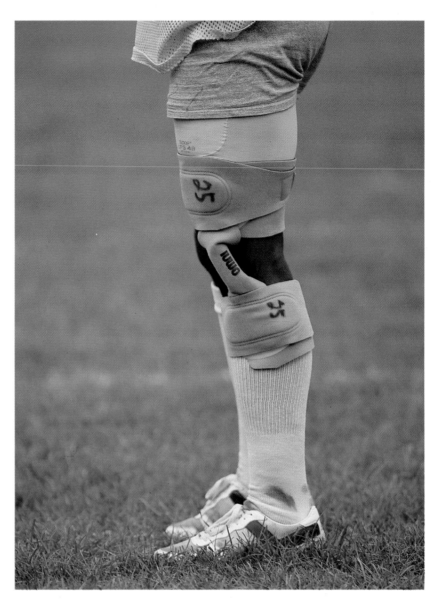

Knees are the axis upon which the football player's life turns. It is not uncommon, despite the recent practice of wearing protective braces, for a player to undergo two or three knee operations in a career.

What It Takes

Harry Carson, the Giants' venerable linebacker, grimaces as he pulls on his underwear. He is a warrior of the highest magnitude and bears the scars of his craft from head to toe.

"I've had concussions, cuts all over my face," Carson says. "My neck hurts. My knees bother me—I've got to keep them loose or they freeze up on me. My shoulder's bad,

I've got sore ribs and my lower back gives me trouble. And then there's the ankle. That's what happens in this game.

"I was talking with a friend of mine who played football for some time and he was saying that everything that hit him, he feels now. Everything. I'm going to have the same problem. Sure, I look okay on the outside, but inside I can feel my bones clanking around."

At the age of thirty-three, Carson is a fairly young man. In the world of professional football, however, he is already an anachronism.

It happens so quickly. The gifted high school athlete is pursued by major colleges and welcomed into the machine. At the age of eighteen he is, essentially, a professional. Tutoring and grooming follow—we know it as college—in many cases lasting for five years. If he is talented and lucky enough, the prospect is drafted by a pro team. If he makes the roster, the player is permitted to wreck havoc on fellow players every Sunday for six months of the year. Violence. Mayhem. All in a day's work.

For this, he is paid handsomely. The game's best athletes draw more than $1 million a season. Even the salaries of journeymen compare favorably with doctors and insurance executives. But at what cost?

The average player lasts four years, or about the time it takes to earn a bachelor of arts degree. Yet, his life is marked indelibly by his time in the game. People want to touch him, listen to him, buy him a drink. The football player is the conduit for all the emotions of those who live vicariously through him. Admittedly, there is a buzz in that.

"When I make a move with the ball and I hear the stadium roar, it's better than sex," says one noted running back. "I mean, you feel electric."

"I wouldn't trade it for anything," Carson says, rubbing his knees. "Then again, maybe I would."

In the old days, the action took place on grass—or in the mud. Today, only eleven teams in the National Football League play on natural fields. The rest play on surfaces the players compare to a trampoline.

The Field

The football field. It's pretty basic: 120 yards long and 53 ⅓ yards wide, with two 10-yard end zones. Goalposts at either end. That's it. Surfaces, of course, vary. And that's where the debate rages.

"I'd like to take the guy who invented artificial turf," says Los Angeles Raiders defensive end Howie Long, "and body-slam him on it twenty-five times. Let's see how he likes that."

The owners like it, to be honest, because vacuuming is far cheaper than mowing, resodding, and fertilizing. The players hate it with a passion usually reserved for bitter rivals.

A research chemist who shall remain nameless found himself fiddling with polymers one day and —poof!— artificial turf was born. It was introduced in 1968 at the Houston Astrodome and has spread like a terminal disease to seventeen of the National Football League's stadiums, going by the name of Astro-Turf, SuperTurf, and—isn't this wonderful?—Texas Turf at the Dallas Cowboys' Texas Stadium. Basically, it is a carpet of green plastic that rests on top of a few inches of padding and six feet of asphalt. Wonderful.

Have you ever suffered the pain of a rug burn after a fall in the living room? It happens every play on artificial turf. Look at the arms of any football player and you can see the damage in terms of welts and sores, many of them permanent. Fortunately, good old-fashioned grass prevails on eleven of the league's fields.

"If a cow can't eat it," baseball player Richie Allen once said, perhaps speaking for his football peers, "I don't want to play on it."

Sure, the football is oddly shaped, and when thrown incorrectly can flop embarrassingly end over end. But when the quarterback releases it in just the right way, it positively *flies*.

The Football

In this game, possession of the football is nine-tenths of the law. Lose it, and lose the game—and perhaps your job.

The center snaps it to the quarterback, who in turn hands it to the running back. Or maybe he throws it to the wide receiver. The eleven offensive players all have the same goal: advance the ball down the field. The eleven defensive players have but one thought: take it away.

"Turnovers," the coach groans after another loss, "cost us the game." Small wonder, for the thing *is* oddly shaped, and therefore *does* take many strange bounces. Its oblong nature distinguishes it from the other, more conventional, objects of pursuit in baseball, basketball, soccer, and golf.

As far back as the late fifteenth century, British lads were known to kick a pig's bladder around village streets for fun. Indians in America did the same. By the late nineteenth century, the bladder was encased in leather. Like everything else in society, the football has grown more sophisticated over the years. Today's version looks like something the Russians might have developed to protect the Kremlin.

When a deft touch is supplied, the football can spiral like a top, its white laces a blur. Conversely, a crude hand—or foot—can send the ball flopping end over end. But as *long* as it gets there, it doesn't really matter *how* it gets there. This is the egalitarian aspect of the game.

Truly, that is the way this weird ball bounces.

Helmets

A guy can become attached to his helmet over the years. In fact, it sometimes can become attached to *him.* Buffalo Bills' guard Jim Ritcher never leaves home without it.

The coaches call them "hats," as in "We're going to have to put our hats on them if we want to win."

That's the coach talking, the man who watches all that brutal contact from the sanctity of the sideline. The player looks at the helmet a little differently.

"It keeps our brains from spilling out," says one. It's hard to tell if he's serious.

The warning, stretched across each helmet in fine print like the surgeon general's on cigarettes, leaves no margin for doubt: "Do not use this helmet to butt, ram, or spear an opposing player. This is in violation of the football rules and can result in severe head, brain, or neck injury, paralysis or death to you and possible injury to your opponent."

And then: "NO HELMET CAN PREVENT ALL SUCH INJURIES."

One imagines linebacker Lawrence Taylor pausing to consider those grim possibilities before he sacks the other team's quarterback. Well, perhaps one can't. As long as the insurance company is satisfied....

Football players wear their hearts on their sleeves and their handles on their heads. The zoological approach is a big favorite. There are Buffaloes thundering across a red plain, Miami Dolphins leaping through a flaming orange hoop, Cardinals, Falcons, Lions, and even Seahawks— whatever they are. The corporate sector is well represented by Houston and Pittsburgh, where oil wells and the steel trademark are the banner carried into war. And history

Players, you may have noticed, often shed their helmets on the sidelines. This is because they are quite painful to wear. To work properly, they have to be snug—and, frankly, most players can't wait to get them off. They say it's because they're too tight, but *we* know their agents tell them that going sans helmet on the sidelines is good for exposure on national television.

repeats itself every Sunday when the Patriots, Redskins, and Chiefs take the field.

The only teams that spell out their names are the Giants, Jets, and Raiders, which says something about the metropolitan fans in New York and Los Angeles. "America's Team," the Dallas Cowboys, wears stars on its helmets, which says something about where their heads are at.

And you can believe the New Orleans Saints hear about their helmets when the big boys knock heads in the trenches. Those Cajuns proudly display the fleur-de-lis, the flower of the lily that declares their ancestry. The Tampa Bay Buccaneers are a little suspect in that respect— their foppish pirate looks less like a swashbuckling Errol Flynn than an unconvincing Peter Pan.

The really good helmet

Teams often take on the characteristics of their helmets. The San Diego Chargers, for example, employ a passing attack that often strikes as quickly as the lightning bolt they proudly wear. Of course, there are times when the Cardinals' play is uh, for the birds.

designs, however, are the most basic, befitting the game itself. The Browns of Cleveland are as imaginative as their name, but their burnt-orange helmets are football's only unsullied lids. The Cincinnati Bengals' tiger stripes are a variation on that theme. Green Bay and Chicago of the NFC's Black-and-Blue Central Division simply sport their initials. The Colts wear a lucky horseshoe, but it hasn't helped them much since they arrived in Indianapolis.

Underneath it all is a football player, and the amalgamation of plastic and steel helps them keep their heads, so to speak. Understandably, players become attached to their helmets. One notable player of a day gone by used to sleep with his. Many use the same one year after year.

And the coach says it's only a hat.

There used to be a time when a player could spit in the privacy of the sidelines. No more, especially with the mushrooming capacity of television and an army of still photographers chronicling his every move. These days, a coach can't even call a meeting without drawing a crowd.

The Sidelines

You can run, but you can't hide. You've just fumbled the football and the team's last chance to win. You've just missed the tackle that would have locked it up. Try to get away. Frank Warren, a defensive end for the New Orleans Saint, tries to disappear by affecting a look of foreign intrigue.

Hi, Mom.

Even in the professional ranks, this is the universal greeting from the sidelines. The camera moves in on the player who has just scored a touchdown, intercepted a pass, recovered a fumble, et cetera. Our hero waves his we're-number-one finger across America's television screens and you can read his lips: Hi, Mom.

The sidelines are just what the name implies—a place to gather yourself away from the fray. A place to reflect, a place to consider... retirement, for one thing.

On the field, it appears that eleven players work as one. Not quite so, for there are eleven individual battles in progress. More often than not, the player's thoughts center around the man across the line of scrimmage he's trying to beat. Mind games are at work here. It's grueling—and yet these are the lucky guys.

Those players who don't play—they're the ones with the clean uniforms—have a more difficult time. Go ahead, try to get excited about the man who beat you out of a job in training camp.

Consider the sidelines a pit stop. Check the water? The Gatorade? Okay under the hood? A little oxygen after a long run? And then they're off the bench again, headed for a few more laps.

Injuries

The physics involved are terrifying.

Take a 230-pound man who can run faster than most of humanity and place him on a collision course with another similar specimen. Linebacker meets running back. Mass times velocity equals mayhem, at the very least. The sheer torque involved is astounding.

Which is why things break. It happens most often at the seams, the joints. Knees, ankles, shoulders, and elbows weren't meant to endure the kind of duress football creates.

Injuries are a way of life in football, a part of the emotional baggage players must carry around with their playbooks. If you play, chances are you're going to get hurt.

Though the roster has room for only forty-five players, there is a taxi-squad of sorts called the Injured Reserve List, and usually five to ten players can be found on it in various states of disrepair. When someone else gets carted off, teams reach into these pools of hobbled talent for backup support.

Knees are the prevailing

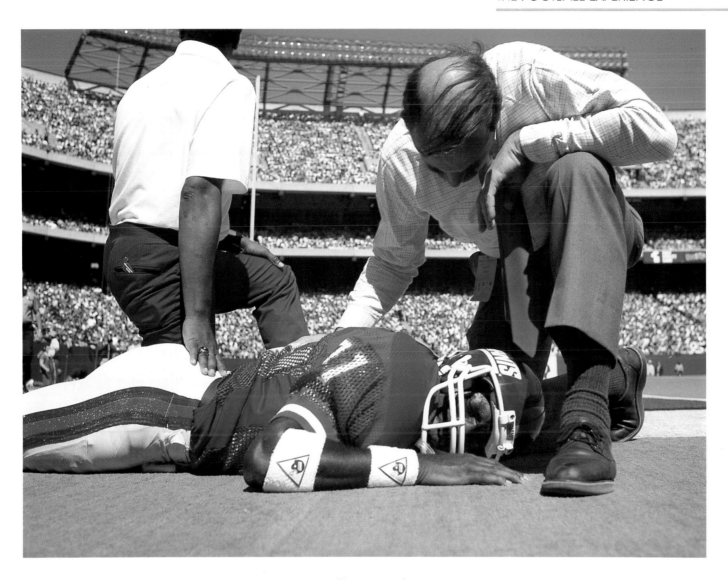

problem. They are a player's fulcrum, his means of mobility. Stopping, starting, cutting—they all place a strain on the delicate knee ligaments. Helmets have an adverse effect, too. Football fans now know the ligaments by name: the medial collateral, the anterior and posterior cruciates. Snap one and flirt with the end of your career.

The road back is a long and painful one. Rehabilitation is a physical and mental healing process. After endless hours on a stationary bicycle, thousands of pounds of weights, can he still take a hit? The lucky ones can. Some never reach that point.

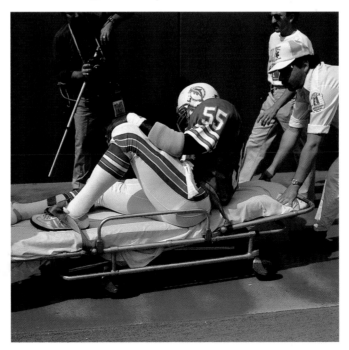

Getting your bell rung in front of 75,000 people can be a humbling experience. "What's your name? Who's your daddy?" the doctors ask. Giants' wide receiver Stacy Robinson, prone (above) was asked where he was playing after a particularly tough shot. "The United States?" he guessed.

There was a time, long, long ago, when pads were for sissies. Now they are necessary equipment— and, tape covers those few vulnerable areas the pads miss. Still, there are occasions when it isn't enough, as Redskins' guard, Ken Huff (right) will tell you.

Darryl Stingley of the New England Patriots had his career—and very nearly his life—ended when he was hit by a streaking Jack Tatum in 1977. He is still paralyzed. Ten years later, Green Bay defensive back Tim Lewis walked away from the game when doctors said another tackle might leave him just as helpless.

As players get bigger, faster, and stronger, the umbrella of preventive medicine seeks to keep pace. Most offensive linemen now wear braces to protect their knees. So do many quarterbacks. Many of the passers also wear flak jackets to keep their ribs intact. Thigh, hip, and shoulder pads are larger and more resilient.

White athletic tape, the old standby, still gets wrapped around ankles. It takes most of a forty-five-foot roll to accomplish the job per player—five days a week for six months—and most teams go through more than seventy miles a season.

If only it worked for knees.

Despite the fact that most players wear about 18 lbs. worth of pads, braces, protectors, and other equipment, injuries occur at a frightening rate.

JOE MONTANA

The San Francisco quarterback was rolling to the left side when he spotted the receiver breaking free far to his right. Still moving left, Joe Montana twisted and threw to the right. He wasn't touched by a single Tampa Bay Buccaneer on the play, but on September 7, 1986, his back began to throb.

Further examination revealed a ruptured disc. His doctors said he'd never play again. Whatever Montana said he kept to himself.

A few days after surgery, he began doing situps in his hospital bed, followed by brief walks. Soon Montana found himself with a football in his hands. He and his wife went to a small park near their Redwood City, California home and Montana threw his first post-surgery passes into a soccer net.

A week later, Montana was back practicing with the team, and on November 9—sixty-five days after sustaining the injury—he started against the St. Louis Cardinals. His doctor, who had warned him not to return to football, couldn't watch. The 49ers won and Montana ultimately led San Francisco to a division title.

It wasn't exactly that easy, though. Montana left the experience a changed man. He no longer takes the risks he once did. Opposing defenses know he is less prone to scramble out of the pocket. That's what happens when your immortality is threatened.

JOE THEISMANN

Joe Theismann didn't have the fastest 40-yard dash time, and he couldn't throw the ball through a wall. All he could do was win. After kicking around the Canadian Football League for a few years, he took Washington, D.C. by storm.

He had taken the Washington Redskins to dizzying heights and now he lay on the ground at RFK Stadium, clutching his shattered right leg.

Joe Theismann, just under six feet tall and weighing two hundred pounds, was the man who had guided Washington to victory in Super Bowl XVII, a game that had been the high-water mark in his twelve-year career with the Redskins—a career that had just ended abruptly on Monday, November 18, 1985, under the harsh glare of national television lights.

He was fading back to pass when Giants linebacker Lawrence Taylor crashed in on a blitz. The two players went down together and when Taylor got up he was cringing. Instinctively gagging at the sight of Theismann laying on the ground, L.T. yanked off his helmet and began screaming for the Redskin trainers.

Theismann never played again. Not to worry, though. It was actually a career break (pun intended) of some magnitude. Theismann made an effort to return to the field, probably to satisfy his $1.4 million insurance policy with Lloyd's of London, but it wasn't to be. He now spends his time with girl-friend-actress Cathy Lee Crosby and does some television work as an analyst.

Theismann's injury demonstrated the regenerative nature of the game. When he left the contest on a stretcher, Washington was trailing the Giants. But an unknown quarterback named Jay Schroeder came in and led the Redskins to victory. Immediately, they began calling him another Theismann.

New York Jets' defensive end, Mark Gastineau, has always been a little extreme—in his play, his sack dances, and even his hair. In 1986, he took the field looking something like Conan the Barbarian.

MARK GASTINEAU

Although he once wrote a book called *The Body You Want,* there are times when Mark Gastineau probably wishes he could trade his in for a 5'7", 135-pound model. Anything to stop that aching in his middle.

A pulled abdominal muscle will do that to you, even if you happen to stand 6'5" and weigh 264 pounds. And that seemingly trivial injury left one of the game's greatest players less than a shadow of himself.

In 1984, the New York Jets' defensive end had sacked opposing quarterbacks twenty-two times, the highest total in history. In 1986, Gastineau failed to tackle a quarterback once. His two sacks were accidents more than anything else.

"I can't go full force at a guy," Gastineau would say, shrugging. "It's the most painful injury I've ever had."

Bent knees, broken thumbs, and groin pulls were never like this. And the only antidote for his invisible injury is rest. When you are paid $800,000 a year to play football, however, that isn't a viable alternative. So Gastineau played at half-speed for a few games before the Jets finally chained him to the sidelines.

"Frustrated isn't the word for it," Gastineau said. "I am completely useless. How would you feel if you couldn't do your job?"

You won't find Larry Bird out here. Baby, it's cold outside—and that's where you'll find football players. When they're not on the field, though, even real men like to snuggle up to those thermonuclear heaters by the bench.

Weather

Get this straight: Real men play football.

They are not tall, anemic-looking, skinny guys running around in shorts in the climate-controlled comfort of an indoor arena. Neither are they squat, stick-wielding fellows who sit in their dressing rooms between periods as someone on a funny machine buffs their indoor ice surface.

And, certainly, this is not a game where the players wear caps and gloves and go home if it rains.

These are real men. Neither ice, nor snow, nor rain, nor sleet stays these couriers from the swift completion of their appointed games. You have seen the pictures, the film clips. Nothing bares the hardy soul of football quite like the elements.

Rain? Nothing special, the player says. Happens all the time. Mud? They'll play with it up to their knees if that is what's necessary. Snow? Great, the coach says. Passing will be impossible. Now we'll see who's really better. Cold?

The most memorable weather game—arguably the most dramatic game in football history—was the championship game between the Green Bay Packers and the Dallas Cowboys played in Green Bay at the end of the 1967 season. They still call it the Ice Bowl, and with good reason. It was sixteen below zero that day at Lambeau Field, and winning may have been secondary to simply surviving.

The Cowboys held a 17-14 lead, but led by quarterback Bart Starr, the Packers moved down the field in the final minutes of the game. With no time outs left and only thirteen seconds on the clock, Starr ran for a one-yard touchdown behind guard Jerry Kramer's crunching block, and Green Bay won 21-17. Two weeks later the Packers won the first Super Bowl, beating Kansas City, 35-10.

Yet after their frozen epic against the Cowboys, the Super Bowl was purely anti-climactic.

You have to want it pretty badly to play— or watch—a game like football on a thoroughly nasty day. There's truly nothing quite like a September day in the rain. Mud guards are, of course, optional.

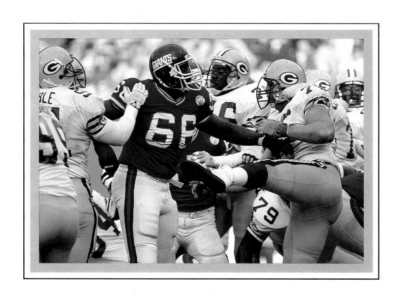

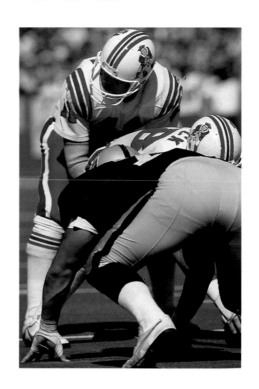

Quarterbacks

This is the guy with the brains and the hefty paycheck to go with them.

And that's as it should be. The quarterback takes the ball from the center on every offensive play and then must decide what to do with it. Simple, huh? Not exactly.

It doesn't always matter which play the coach sent in, or which one was called in the huddle. Circumstances change quickly on the football field and quarterbacks are paid handsomely to stay one step ahead of the opposition. They read the defense—the blitzing linebacker, the roaming free safety, the stunting linemen—and react. It all happens in less than three seconds. In that scant time, championships are won and lost.

The common denominator among great quarterbacks is confidence. Call it cockiness, guts, or something unprintable. Jim McMahon of the Chicago Bears wears his confidence on his sleeve, not to mention his headband. How many players in the NFL would tell the commissioner to get lost, much less get away with it? He tells you what he's going to do, and then does it. Others, such as Miami's Dan Marino and Denver's John Elway, lead by the example set by their arms, not their mouths. Whatever it takes in this game.

They may spend more time in front of the mirror than most of their teammates, but they deserve that luxury. Quarterbacks, after all, take a fierce beating. There aren't many who make it through a whole season intact. They are the targets of all those blitzes, and raging outside linebackers like nothing better than to dust opposing quarterbacks.

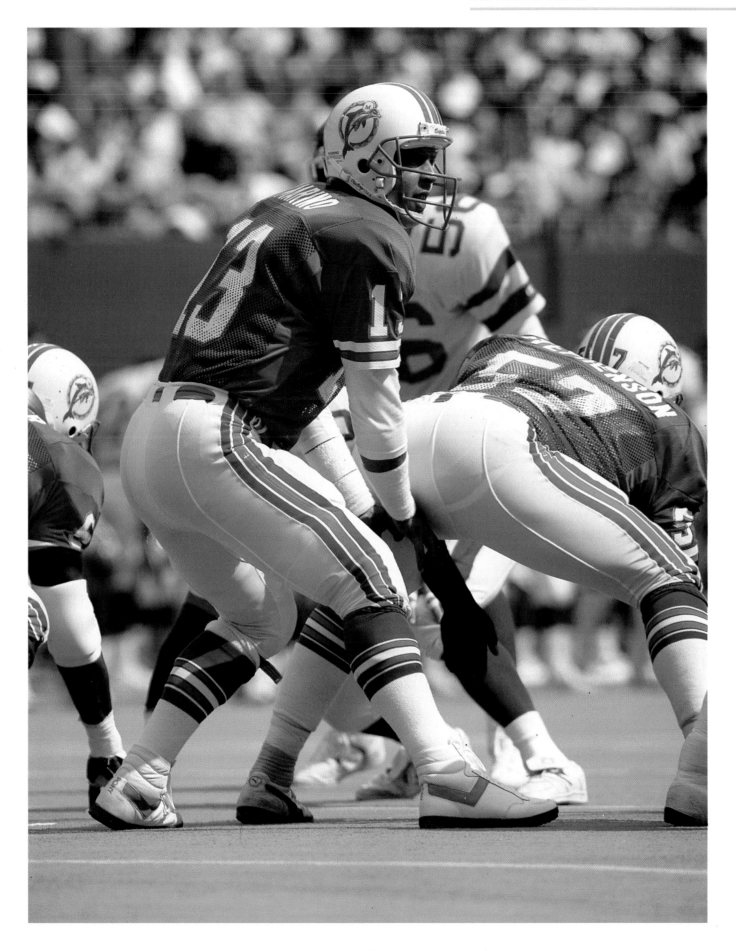

Off the field, being a quarterback is just as tough—maybe tougher. The debate begins every season in training camp, and there is no let-up by the fans or media. Should X really be the starter? The only rule of thumb is that the backup always looks better because he's not out there screwing up. Of course, when the backup becomes the starter the statute of limitations runs out. That's when the third-stringer starts looking pretty good. When he starts screwing up, well…there's always next year.

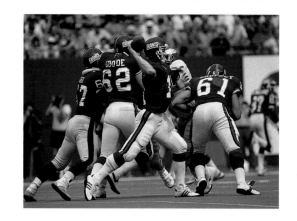

Behold Phil Simms (left) the courageous quarterback for the New York Giants. Injured four straight years, he remained convinced that he wasn't injury-prone, and his 1986 Pro Bowl and 1987 Super Bowl MVP awards proved him right. At the age of thirty, Simms still seems to be getting better, if that is possible.

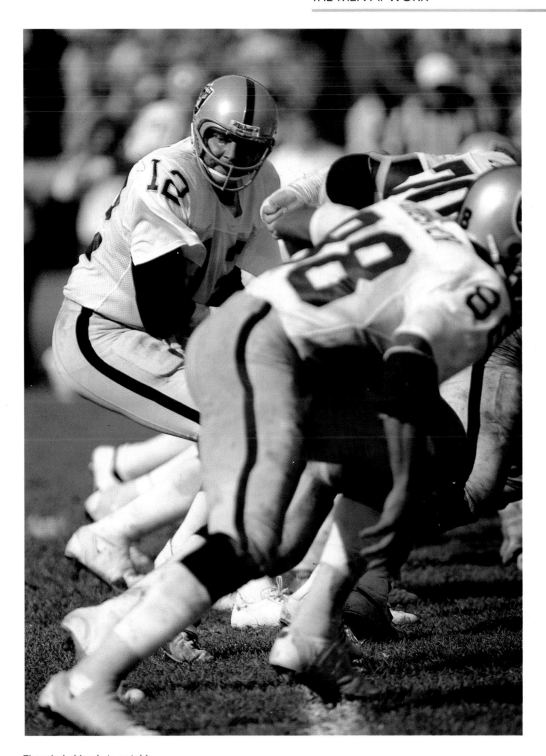

The whole idea is to get rid of the ball before the defense can catch you with it, as Los Angeles Ram, Jim Everett (left) demonstrates by pitching out to Eric Dickerson. Ken Stabler (top) of the Los Angeles Raiders is also trying to think of a way out.

Receivers

They float through the defensive secondary like butterflies—then sting like a bee when the football finally arrives.

The quarterback launches the ball and the receiver launches himself in an effort to reel it in. More than any other player, the wide receiver is a ballet dancer. Gracefully, he follows the choreographer's steps. Ideally, he arrives at the same point in time as the football.

Wide receivers generally fall into two categories: burners and possession receivers.

Burners, as you might suspect, are *faaaast.* They fly down the sideline with little thought of finesse or fakes. San Francisco's Jerry Rice has no peer as he sails past opposing cornerbacks. Chicago's Willie Gault was

It's no coincidence that wide receivers look like track men crouching in their starting blocks before the big sprint—that's really what they are. On your mark, get set, go! Run a post-pattern that leaves the defensive back in your dust. Some wide receivers, like Darren Long of the Los Angeles Rams, who also doubles as a tight end, can even catch the ball.

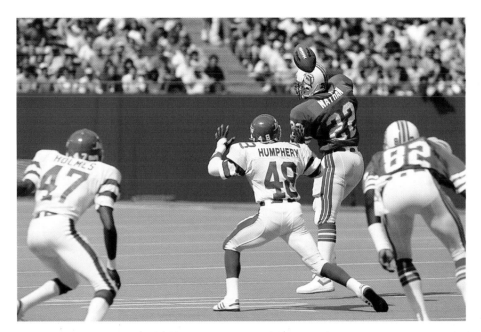

Most offensive players are expected to have some kind of hand-eye coordination when it comes to catching the ball. Miami's Tony Nathan demonstrates how difficult it can be when defensive players join the effort. He knows it's hard enough to succeed in this business without someone crashing the party.

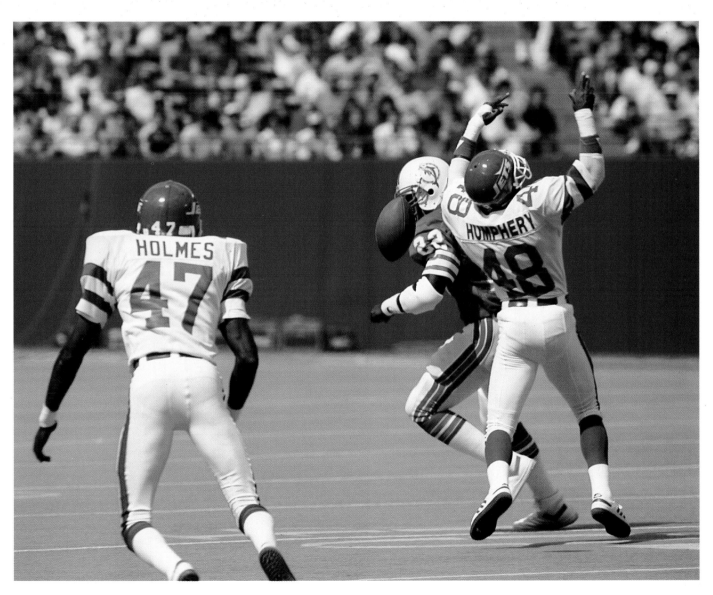

Although individual styles vary, the best receivers outrun, outmaneuver, or just plain overpower their opponent. It doesn't matter how, just as long as they catch the ball. That's why they're called receivers.

once a world-class hurdler. Al Toon of the Jets takes long, loping strides. Washington's Gary Clark is tiny and elusive but just as dangerous. James Lofton of Green Bay glides under the ball.

The possession receivers do not have speed as an ally. Instead, guile and craftiness are their weapons. Steve Largent of Seattle has no speed to speak of, but his hands are as soft as velvet. That Largent has caught passes in more consecutive games than any receiver ever is a testament to his efficiency. He doesn't look like much; all he does is catch the ball.

Tight ends are an entirely different breed. Not only do they catch the ball, they also are asked—gasp!—to block. Needless to say, they exhibit more character on the field than other players. Or does the tight end position merely field more characters?

Mark Bavaro of the Giants is the prototype these days. He plays football the way they used to back during the Ice Age, catching the short pass and carrying linebackers for dozens of extra yards. Then he knocks the secondary on their behinds.

Actually, tight ends are really just linebackers who happen to catch the ball once in a while. To be honest, some of them would *rather* block.

Linemen

You don't see too many offensive or defensive tackles doing commercials for cologne.

Life in the trenches is a dirty job, to be sure, but somebody's got to do it. Glamorous it isn't. The ball is snapped and the mayhem begins. Grunts. Groans. An elbow to the helmet. A fist somewhere a little lower.

Linemen are football's foot soldiers. They do not carry the ball, except by accident. They do not catch it, unless someone makes the gross mistake of throwing it to them. They are not pretty. In high school, they were called "Moose," or "Grunt," or "Monster," or "Animal." The necks are the tip-off. Is that a neck, or just another set of shoulders?

Size is not a variable here, only shape. The closer you get to the middle of the line, the squatter they get. Centers and the men they block, nose tackles, are built more or less like bowling balls. They line up in front of each other and have at it.

"Being a nose tackle," says Cleveland's Bob Golic, "is like being a fire hydrant at a dog show."

You get the idea.

Guards lead the play for the running backs, and the defensive tackles follow if they can. Offensive tackles, charged with preventing the defensive ends from damaging the quarterback, spend most of their time backpedaling.

Of all the line positions, defensive end is the most visible. It's hard to miss the Jets' Mark Gastineau, "Too Tall" Jones of the Cowboys, the Bears' Richard Dent, or Howie Long of the Los Angeles Raiders.

But they're exceptions to the rule. Like Golic, most linemen are just hard-working fire hydrants trying to make a living.

There is a sort of premeditated insanity about line play. The coach draws the play in August, then in November, when it really means something, you have to knock your man off his feet. It's as simple as that.

The degree of specialization, as you might imagine, is magnified on special teams. The long snapper must deliver a bullet in the hands of the punter or holder from an upside-down position. The kick returner has it easy. He just has to catch the ball.

Special Teams

This is the crème de la crème of crazy. Why do you think they call football's special teams units "suicide squads?"

The kickoff is in the air. The ten players—the kicker sort of trots along, hoping the runner never makes it to him—run at full bore for thirty, forty, fifty yards and then try to find someone to knock over. The very best specialists move with a controlled abandon.

Intelligent recklessness, whatever *that* is, seems to be the quality necessary to be successful on special teams.

The specials player intent on the tackle tries not to think about the reserve linebacker who makes his only game appearances for these berserk five-second flashes or the backup who makes his entire living on dangerous kick runback teams. These are guys you want to keep an eye on.

Football has done its best to police this violent area of the game. Blocking rules have been tightened up, and more elaborate schemes for protecting the kick returner have been devised. Still, the concept gives one pause.

Here (in some cases) is a college graduate making $150,000 a year as a "wedge-buster." That's what they call the player who hurls himself into the protective wall in front of the runner. He's the quintessential special teams player. When the players fall, sometimes like bowling pins, the second wave swoops in and makes a tackle. The wedge-buster limps off the field, checking to see if all his fingers are still there. All guts, no glory. He has done his job.

What is the defense thinking when the field goal team comes out on the field? Block that kick. Although the odds of that are hopelessly against them, the defense try to motivate themselves. Although it happens rarely, a blocked kick can turn a game around in a hurry.

What do you call a running back who can bench press 85 lbs. more than his own weight, run the 40-yard dash in 4.5 seconds, and walk 40 yards on his hands? Some call him "Sweetness," but Walter Payton (left) is his name.

Running Backs

On television, they call these guys the talent. In football, they are known merely as running backs. Here is the ball, the quarterback says, take it somewhere. The good ones oblige. Style often supercedes substance.

Walter Payton scampers. He really does. The Chicago halfback bounces down the sideline, his legs splaying out at delightful angles. No one has carried the ball for more yards in the NFL than Payton. "Sweetness" is his nickname, but when he knocks a strong safety off his feet, you have to wonder why.

Eric Dickerson of the Los Angeles Rams may one day surpass Payton as the best at his craft. Dickerson runs with a different kind of élan. His is a style that capitalizes on his frightening—if you're a defense player—combination of size, speed, and strength.

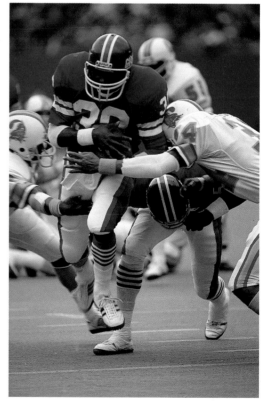

Here he comes, here he comes...there he goes. The Move has been rendered and the running back is gone. Or is he? Sometimes it works, sometimes it doesn't. It is that element of doubt that keeps the game interesting.

And then there is Joe Morris of the Giants. Only five-seven, Morris has the strongest set of legs on the team. All his life he had been told he wasn't good enough or big enough. Now he is one of football's most exciting runners. His off-tackle jags aren't recommended for weak hearts.

Those are some of the league's best halfbacks. Fullbacks are a little less spectacular and they spend most of their time blocking. Sometimes they're allowed to catch the ball out of the backfield. But when a single yard is required to keep a drive alive, the fullback usually gets the call. He may lumber, but a yard is a yard.

And that's the point. They all do it differently, but they do it. Give him a leg, take it away. A head fake, a hip swivel, whatever it takes. Or just run your opponent over. Just get the ball—and take it down the field.

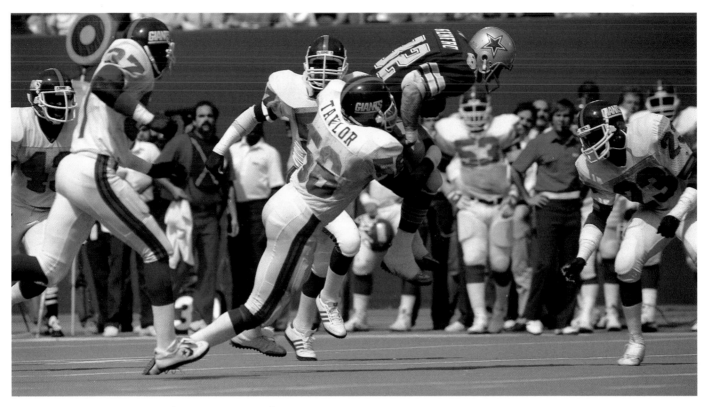

Linebackers

Linebackers, a wise man once said, play football in an ill humor. That is all you need to know about linebackers. They are mean and nasty and represent everything that football was intended to be. Do not, if you can help it, allow your daughter to marry one.

Many of the good teams build their defense around three or four good linebackers. They, more than other defensive players, are in a position to determine the outcome of the game because they perform a dual role, rushing the passer *and* running. Since they are sandwiched between the defensive line and the defensive backs, linebackers are asked to do a lot of everything.

The Giants' Lawrence Taylor, for instance, rushes the quarterback most of the time. So do André Tippett of the New England Patriots and Chip Banks of Cleveland. It's a task that usually falls to outside linebackers, since, as a group, they are a little faster, a little lighter. Inside linebackers, on the other hand, control the opponent's running game. Chicago's Mike Singletary and Harry Carson of the Giants are among the best.

The truly great linebackers succeed by sheer force of will. Pittsburgh's Jack Lambert, he of the spooky toothless grin, was like that. So was Chicago's Dick Butkus and Green Bay's Ray Nitschke.

The frenzy they create is legendary. In terms of physics, linebackers are the most dangerous players on the field. Their size and speed make them so. Quarterbacks hate them—with good reason.

Their daughters will never find out why.

Remember the guy who used to tear up telephone books in high school? That is the sort who grows up to become a linebacker. Today, the biggest and baddest is the Giants' legendary Lawrence Taylor (above and left).

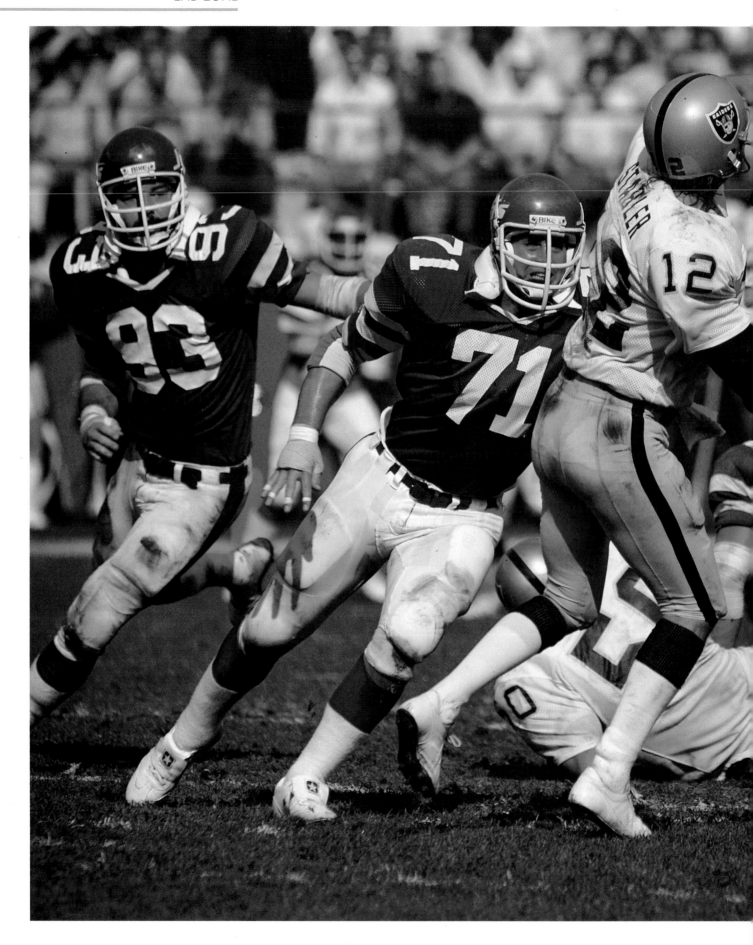

Linebackers (like Harry Carson, below) are menacing fellows. Ken Stabler, (left, on the run) formerly of the Raiders, can tell you about that. Never, he will tell you, never socialize with linebackers—on or off the field. They can be hazardous to your health.

The Buffalo Bills' punter, John Kidd, demonstrates the vulnerability all kickers in the National Football League exhibit on any given Sunday. The trick is to get that right leg down before the linemen arrive.

Kickers

These guys aren't really football players. Are they? No. Football's kickers are a necessary evil, as far as the rest of the players are concerned. They don't block, they don't tackle—have you ever seen a kicker start running the other way when an opposing runner heads in his direction? And God forbid they should throw it. Remember Miami's Garo Yepremian in Super Bowl VII, whose field goal attempt never got off the ground, forcing him to try a pass of sorts? Washington's Mike Bass picked it out of the air and raced forty-nine yards for the Redskins' only touchdown of the day. That's why they call it "foot"-ball.

Theirs is primarily a head game. For here are 5'9", 155-pound types who spend most of their time on the sidelines watching the big boys bash it out. Then, with the game on the line, they come trotting in with their clean little uniforms—to win or lose it. No wonder kickers are a little neurotic.

They spend the week hanging around waiting for Sunday. While the rest of the players are practicing hard, placekickers do crossword puzzles, ride stationary bicycles, or play cards with the clubhouse boys. They do not sweat much.

The placekicker endures more mental pressure than any other player on the team, however. Most kickers practice some form of previsualization or indulge in concentration exercises. The Giants' Raul Allegre actually watches films of his greatest kicks to put him in the right frame of mind.

One thing about placekickers: they never miss a kick. At least not without some help. The snap was bad. The hold was bad. The turf was loose. The wind took it. Right.

Punters have a less glorious function—they clean up after the elephants. When the offense fails to gain a first down, the punter bails the team out. Hopefully. His job is to control field position with spiraling mortar-shots.

Practice, practice, practice. That's how Miami's Reggie Roby became one of the best in the business. He used to spend his childhood days kicking a football over his family's house, from the backyard to the front, and back again, over and over, all day long.

Now, that's weird. Unless, of course, you are a kicker.

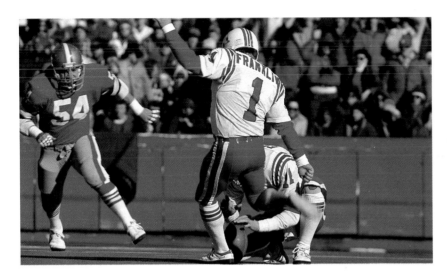

As Tony Franklin of the New England Patriots illustrates, a kicker is usually alone with his thoughts and his holder. Chris Bahr (below) of the Los Angeles Raiders sends the ball up and over a sea of bodies.

They are hopelessly perky, but that's all part of the job description. Indeed, the cheerleader is more ornamental than anything else. But then, blocking and tackling is not a prerequisite.

The Cheerleader

Cheerleader: *n. A person who leads others in cheering for a team, as at football games.*

That's how *Webster's Dictionary* describes those sprites of the sidelines, but when was the last time you heard something like "Go team!" or "Push 'em back, push 'em back, waaay back!" at a professional football game?

That, a course, is not the point. Long ago, football discovered the credo that Madison Avenue lives by: give the fan a pretty face and he'll be easily led for four quarters.

Oh, sure, the purists cringe. They say football already has all the pathos and drama a game could want. Some teams simply will not tolerate cheerleaders on the sidelines, preferring instead some lumpy mascot or a looney banging on a drum. But who isn't moved when the lineups are announced and those heavily rouged cheeks bounce out onto the field? Flash. Dash. Color. Pageantry. Flying, uh, pom-poms. Truly, they are visions to behold. Just don't expect any wildly talented, soon-to-be stars or particularly sound choreography. Again, that isn't the point. Pom-poms are the point.

The Dallas Cowboys generally credit themselves with rediscovering cheerleaders in the modern era, which is not surprising. In 1972, they introduced the "new" Dallas Cowboys Cheerleaders, who sported cute little white boots, fringed vests, short-shorts, and enough cleavage to command even the weakest attention span. Their names, over the years, invariably have

ended in vowels: Kelli, Misty, Tiffany, Krista, Courtney, Lindsay, Kari. They are usually aerobics instructors, or secretaries, or flight attendants. At some point—probably Super Bowl X in Miami's Orange Bowl—they "captured the imagination of a nation," according to the Dallas media guide.

Maybe so. The Dallas Cowboys Cheerleaders have traveled the globe, sharing their "beauty and talent" with everyone they meet. As a result of their success, the '70s spawned a number of cheerleading units throughout football. In cities where sellouts are not the norm, they are an acknowledged drawing card.

Sometimes, they draw more stares than they're supposed to. Linebacker Rickey Jackson of the New Orleans Saints was once fined by his coach for spending more time concentrating on the backfields in motion on the sidelines than the game at hand. It happens more often than you think.

The players will also tell you that the imitators are better than the real thing. "The Dallas Cheerleaders are so overrated," one says. "They've got the reputation, but when the game is on the line, I'll take the girls in Miami or Atlanta. At least they're coordinated. Philadelphia has a lot of potential, too."

Indeed, an informal poll of the players rates the cheerleaders in Miami and Atlanta as the crème de la crème. On the other hand, the units in St. Louis and New England need some help.

Geography plays an important role. Warm-weather cities seem to have the recruiting edge—at any rate, their cheerleaders wear less.

The days of "Push 'em back, push 'em *waaay* back" are long gone. Today's cheerleaders put together some pretty high-tech routines. This is not to say that they are always in step together. But, at the very bottom, who cares?

The Officials

Whether you call it decision by committee, or strength in numbers, it's a safe bet the zebras will *always* converge before making important announcements.

They come from good homes and good jobs.

During the week, they work as oil company executives, insurance salesmen, bankers, and commercial real estate brokers. And then, ever on a Sunday, football's officials can't seem to do anything right. They are fine men, really. Why, then, doesn't anyone in this game like them?

"You can take all those guys in stripes and send them to the end of the world," the coach says after a particularly tough loss, or words to that effect.

"The zebras got us today," the player explains, shaking his head. "They wouldn't call holding if there was an octopus out there."

Their eyesight, their ancestry, is questioned on a weekly basis. Yet they usually handle these assaults on their character with humor and aplomb. The reason may be their unique perspective on the sport. Football does not employ its officials full-time. Unlike baseball umpires and referees in basketball and hockey, football's men in stripes do not depend on the game for a living.

Nevertheless, the eight-man team is judge and jury in all disputes. The referee—the players and coaches will point out that he's the one with the black hat—runs the show. He is backed by the umpire, the head linesman, the line judge, the back judge, the side judge, the field judge, and the

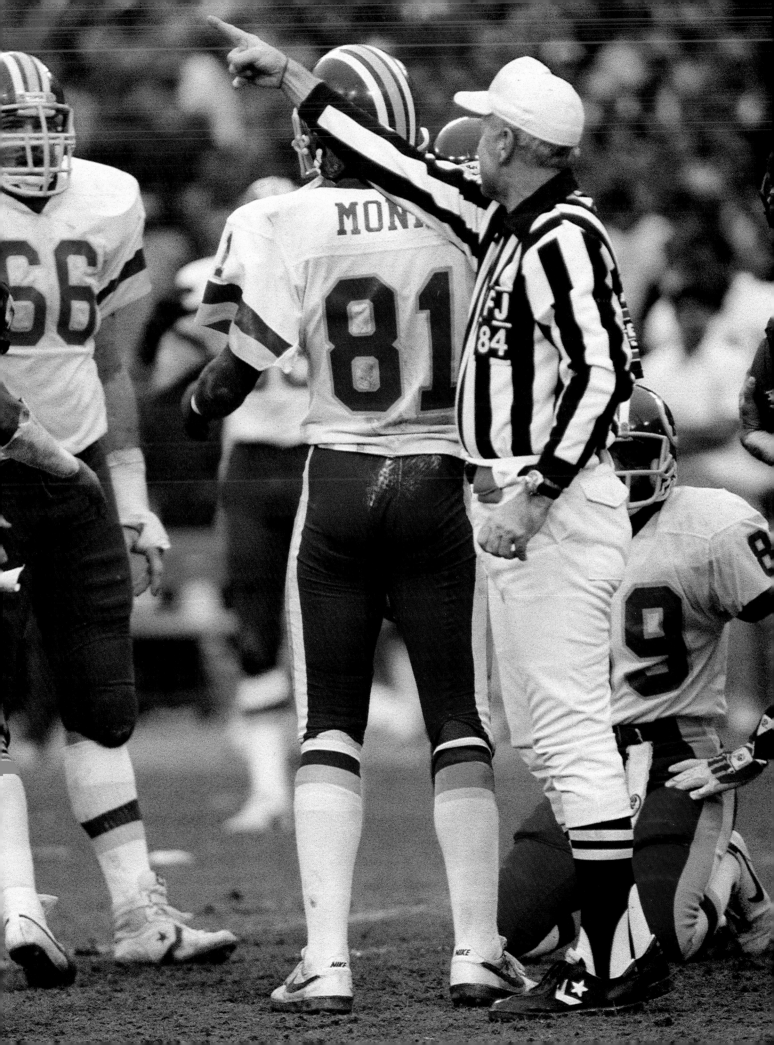

Bob McElwee (No. 95) is in control here. He is wired into the replay official, who looms high above the field in the press box, and wired into the television production unit with the latest in microphone technology. But that's only on Sunday. The rest of the week, McElwee runs his own construction company. It's all the same: laying foundations and making sure the game is up to code.

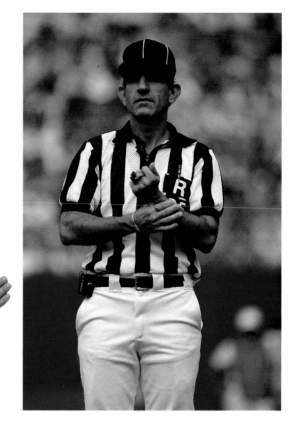

replay official up in the press box. They all enforce the rules of the game, but the referee has the most fun, because he's the one who goes through the motions for the crowd and the folks at home watching television. It's his way of explaining what just happened.

The most familiar signal, of course, is the arms extended above the head, indicating that a touchdown has been scored or that a kick has been successful. Notice the official's impassive face on such a joyous occasion. He has been trained not to betray a trace of elation, even if his favorite team just scored.

Among other signals, there is the conventional first-down thrust, the self-explanatory holding call, and familiar signs for offsides and an incomplete pass. And then it gets interesting.

You can be penalized for encroachment, lining up in the neutral zone, intentional grounding, and—goodness—

a dead-ball foul. Illegal use of hands and unsportsmanlike conduct are two other crimes punishable by five, ten, or fifteen yards. It hardly seems like enough, if the descriptions are even remotely accurate.

Watch the officials closely when the cameras permit it. They are often as entertaining as the plays and the players themselves. The ad-libs— "That's fifteen yards, he's giving him the business"—can be priceless.

Considering the simmering emotions that dominate the football field, the officials exercise a fair degree of control. In some cases, the players weigh twice as much as the officials. Then, again... like the players, officials are listed by their college. Heights and weights, however, are nowhere to be found. Some of those oil company executives and insurance salesmen are a little over their playing weights.

Why do you think those stripes are always vertical?

Coaches

You've seen this look of scrutiny before. What are these men (from left to right) the Giants' Bill Parcells, former Houston Oilers' Coach Bum Phillips, Dallas Cowboys' longtime Coach Tom Landry, and Don Shula of the Miami Dolphins, looking at? Are they worried about their Christmas shopping? Maybe they're thinking about next year's tax returns, or where to put those new shrubs? Perhaps not.

They say air-traffic controllers have the world's toughest jobs, but a day in the tower would be a breeze for a National Football League coach.

He is responsible for more than fifty players—twice the number any other professional sport offers—and all their day-to-day problems. "There are," says Miami coach Don Shula, "a lot of easier things to do with your life."

Perhaps so.

"It's not like any other business," says Giants coach Bill Parcells. "There are no profit margins, no ninety-percent operating ratios. You won or you lost. That is the bottom line in coaching."

Parcells should know. In his first year as head coach, the Giants won three of sixteen games, and Parcells barely lived to tell about it. He survived, however, and since that horrific 1983 season, the

Giants have been a perennial playoff team, finally winning the big one—Super Bowl XXI—in January 1987. Parcells did it his way, with a combination of bluster and bravado, hubris and humility. "The challenge in athletics," he says, "is to get a team to play as close to its potential as you can. That's the quest. I do what I think the situation calls for."

They all do, these twenty-eight men on twenty-eight islands.

Chicago's Mike Ditka, for example, bullied his way to victory in Super Bowl XX, while San Francisco coach Bill Walsh finessed his way there the year before.

Though the good ones come from different molds, they all know how to win. Take Dallas' Tom Landry. He was a defensive back with the Giants and through the years his knowledge grew. Landry

finally invented the "Flex Defense," and it carried the Cowboys to heights they had never reached.

Landry's modus operandi is quiet control. No tantrums or outbursts on the sideline. Under his classic fedora, flexing cheek muscles are the only thing that betray his emotion. On the other hand, Bum Phillips, who spent some time coaching a few miles away in Houston, wore his heart on his bigger-than-Texas ten-gallon hat. Most coaches go for the two-piece suit or the regulation team sweater—but not Bum. There he'd be, stalking the sideline with his ostrich-skin boots and sheepskin jacket. The common denominator with his crossstate rival? Phillips knew how to motivate football players.

Take Don Coryell. He is an offensive genius; in Coryell's heaven there are only zone defenses, which make it easier to win with the passing game—something Coryell lived (and died) with for years in San Diego. Tom Flores of the Los Angeles Raiders is another coach who leans toward offense. He understands the quarterback because he was in the same shoes once, leading the old AFL in pass-completion percentage when he played for the Raiders back in 1960. The Jets' Joe Walton was an end for the Giants. Chuck Noll, a fixture in Pittsburgh, played guard and linebacker for the Cleveland Browns. Others, like John Mackovic of Kansas City and Washington's Joe Gibbs, didn't play professional football at all. They entered the coaching ranks immediately after college as graduate assistants.

"It doesn't matter who you are or where you have been," Bill Parcells says. "Just get the job done."

Over the years, coaches learn to hone the impassive look. Note the intensity of the eyes. Only the accessories differ. Parcells is your basic headset and windbreaker guy; Phillips oozes with cowboy chic; Landry looks like he ought to be selling stocks and bonds; and Shula is always the model of coaching cool. No matter what he's wearing, he looks good. Like all these men, he coaches that way, too.

Coach or college professor? Although Bill Walsh may look like the latter, there can be no doubt—the man is a coach. He puts together some nice offenses, and some of his individual plays are breathtaking. Many a defensive coordinator, gushing all the way, runs Walsh's creations forward and back in the film room, marveling at his genius.

BILL WALSH

He was the first one they called a genius.

The year was 1981 and the San Francisco 49ers stood atop the football world after winning Super Bowl XVI. Bill Walsh had the look—the shaggy white hair, the sensitive eyes, the requisite turtleneck. Hardly Vince Lombardi, but then again this was the '80s.

The résumé looked good, too. Though Walsh had never played football, he had worked under Al Davis in Oakland in 1966. Over the years, quarterbacks became his specialty and he eventually developed Ken Anderson in Cincinnati and, later, Dan Fouts in San Diego. In 1978, Walsh moved to august Stanford University and produced two NCAA passing champions, Guy Benjamin and Steve Dils.

The 49ers hired him in 1979 and Walsh promptly won two of fourteen games. A rookie quarterback named Joe Montana and the rookie coach learned a lot that year. Together, they won six games the next season. Somewhere in three, Walsh became a genius. It didn't last long, however. After winning the Super Bowl in 1981, San Francisco struggled to a 3-6 record the following season. But two seasons later, the 49ers were champions of Super Bowl XIX, and Walsh, who won the title on familiar Stanford soil, was hailed as a genius again. All in all, he handled the transformation pretty well.

"I can't wait," said Walsh, "until next year."

MIKE DITKA

The man has never changed appreciably. If Mike Ditka didn't like to lose when he played in the NFL, he likes it even less now that he's a coach.

Ditka was the NFL's Rookie of the Year in 1961 under legendary Chicago coach George Halas. In 1964, he set a record for catches by a tight end that held up for sixteen years. Ditka went to the Pro Bowl five times and ultimately played twelve years in the league. He had the perfect temperament for a player, explosive yet cool.

That was why when Halas hired him in 1982 critics wondered if Ditka could handle the job. For nine years he had helped coach the Dallas Cowboys' offense under the calming influence of Tom Landry. But his own show? Would he last a week?

In 1982, he lasted the whole 3-6 season. A year later, Chicago won half of its sixteen games. In 1984, the Bears reached the NFC Championship Game. One season later, they dominated the entire league. Chicago, the youngest team in football, won eighteen of nineteen games, and Super Bowl XX was merely the pièce de résistance.

Along the way there was a burst blood vessel or two. A broken hand after a losing encounter with a locker. Threats to players, some of them that turned into promises.

Halas would have smiled. He, too, had played for the Bears and was known for his temper. And Coach Halas didn't win six world championships with his eyes closed. In Ditka, Halas would have seen himself that Super Bowl Sunday.

For when the Chicago Bears were once again crowned champions of the world, on January 26, 1986, Ditka had come full circle. "This one," he said through damp eyes, "was for Mr. Halas."

Gruff. Mean. Nasty. Even with a flashy new permanent, Mike Ditka still looks like a bear. And this Bear is the primary reason that Chicago won Super Bowl XX. Ditka simply bullied the Bears to the title by the sheer force of his will, just as old George Halas knew he would.

SkyCam

It was a noble experiment, to be sure.

The sky camera—or SkyCam as the networks called it—offered a new perspective on football, a bird's-eye view, the catbird seat, the place no camera had ever dared to go before.

A Philadelphia man named Garrett Brown had developed the idea and sold it to the television networks. Truly, it was a director's dream because it could go anywhere at any time. Remote-controlled, The SkyCam could be raised, lowered, tilted, and so on.

Wwwwzzzzzzzz...it would fly high above players' heads on four cables attached to the corners of the stadium. A terrific bit of technical innovation, actually. Except that the price wasn't right.

All three major television networks experimented with SkyCam for several years but the thrill disappeared after a few of those $35,000 bills rolled in, mostly for the cable installation.

They made a brave effort to commercialize SkyCam, to make it a smaller version of the Goodyear blimp—the Pepsi SkyCam, if you will—but it failed. And so SkyCam sits on the shelf, like Joe Namath's white shoes, a fleeting piece of football history.

Training Camp

Certainly, men were not created to play football during the summer. It's a tough enough game without adding heat and humidity to the equation. But in the crucible of July and August are championships won.

Charleston, Illinois. Thousand Oaks, California. Greeley, Colorado. Smithfield, Rhode Island. Pleasantville, New York. Platteville, Wisconsin. Latrobe, Pennsylvania. This is where the National Football League's teams put together the building blocks of a successful season. Or the reverse. There is an intriguing dichotomy at work here. Veterans struggle to hang on; rookies try to push them out of the league. The vicious sounds of football careers beginning and ending reverberate in the pastoral surroundings.

Oddly enough, the coaches probably work harder than any of the hundred-odd players trying to earn one of forty-five roster spots. A mistake can haunt them for a career. Todd Christensen, for example, billed as a fullback out of college, slipped through several training camp nets in 1979 before the Los Angeles Raiders recognized his talent in another area. He is now the standard by which other tight ends are judged.

Rookies have a lot more to prove, so they sweat more than the veterans, though even those first-year players operate within their own caste system. The first-round draft choices preen in front of the locker-room mirror when they're not counting their millions. Their agents have accomplished what they were paid

Belly up to the bar, son, it's time to work. The games are still weeks away, but the price must be paid now if success is the goal. Stretch out that hamstring, my man, it is going to be a *long* and tough season.

twenty percent for—securing their client a comfortable contract bulging with incentives and annuities. Making the team is almost an afterthought.

Even second- and third-round picks are driving around in BMWs and Mercedes. The guys with the Jeeps are free agents. No one drafted them, no pedigree is going to help them. They're the ones who won't go out for beers after practice because they have to study the playbook.

Training camp is not fun.

The veterans understand this and do their best to minimize their time and effort there. Particularly crafty veterans will avoid all or part of camp by holding out for a better contract. "Saves the wear and tear on my legs," says Giants defensive end George Martin, whose legs may

or may not be of the Paleolithic Era. "You learn over the years to become more efficient."

Conditioning is the byword at training camp, although the players have another name for it. For six or seven weeks, running is the bane of their existence. They slog through the one-mile run and the shuttle drills, and concentrate on breathing as they do this, because it's easy to lose yourself in the romance that is training camp.

Weight lifting is another area that gets full attention before the season starts. This appeals to most players, who, after all, are pretty macho fellows. The rookie bench-presses 225 pounds thirty times and the veteran whistles. Then he steps in and throws the bar up there thirty-one times—and staggers off behind

the clubhouse to recover.

Teaching is the other function of training camp. Individual technique gets a lot of attention. All the moves, all the instincts you see unfolding on a football field in December, have been carefully programmed. If you do something often enough, it becomes second nature—even if there's a 300-pound tackle bearing down on you against a backdrop of 70,000 screaming spectators. Thus, the quarterback reads a man-to-man defense and throws to the receiver drawing single coverage; the cornerback backpedals just so.

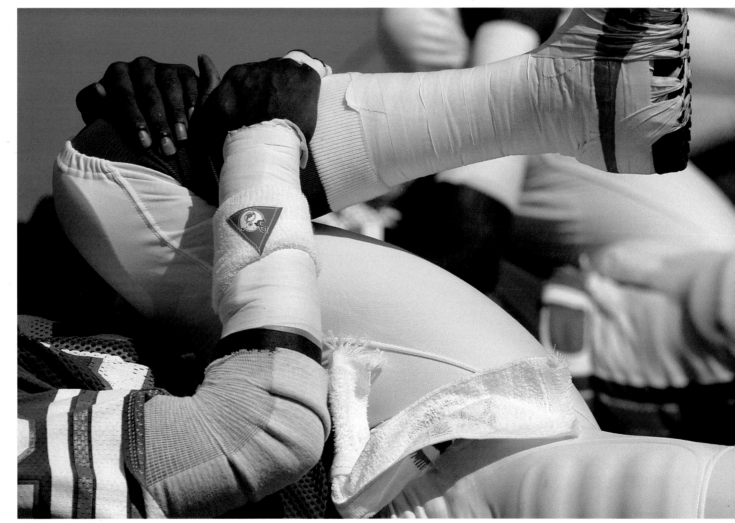

Training camp means exercise, scrimmages, wind sprints, and other such fun, more often than not in hot and humid weather. The players enjoy it as much as might be expected.

Then again, when the coach doesn't like it...

Those are the so-called skill-position players. They're permitted to practice their moves against other players. The hulking men in the trenches, on the other hand, spend a lot of their time trying to move inanimate objects. Blocking sleds. Tackling dummies. When they've got it right, they vent their wrath on each other.

Quite often the anxiety at training camp manifests itself in a fight. The rookie, worried about making the team, lashes out when the veteran elbows him once too often. They lock up, and their teammates are in no hurry to separate them. The coach turns away, smiling; he has seen the spark he was looking for.

There are always a few prospects who can't take the heat and leave of their own accord. The challenge is too great, they miss their sweethearts, they want to get a head start on that job with the trucking firm. And then there are those players who just don't know when to leave.

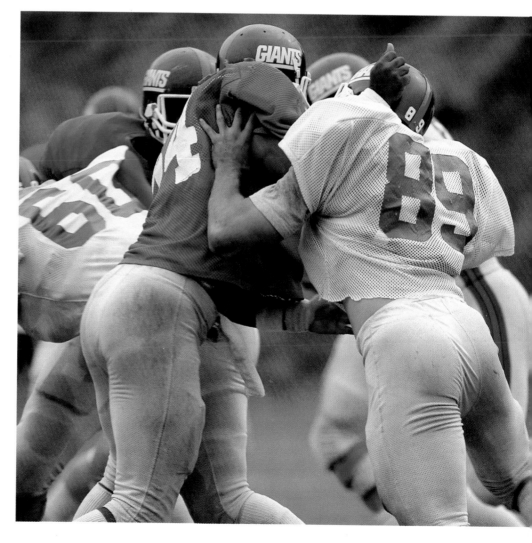

In training-camp lore there is no villain quite like The Turk. He is usually an assistant coach or second-echelon administrator who knocks softly on a player's dormitory door sometime before the sun comes up. "Coach wants to see you." The player knows he is about to be cut. Hiding under the bed won't work, though it has been tried. Running won't work, either. When Charon comes to ferry you to the underworld, arguing is folly. Or is it?

Back in 1975, a small-town unknown-college hero named Kevin O'Brien felt the sting of The Turk at the Giants' training camp. A week earlier, he had signed a free-agent contract and his town had given him a parade and a huge send-off. Now he was history.

On his knees and through tears, O'Brien begged Coach Bill Arnsparger not for another chance, but merely another week. "Coach," he sobbed, "you've got to let me stay another week. It's too embarrassing. They'll never understand."

Arnsparger, to that point an unyielding man, understood. O'Brien stayed for another week. When the time came, he thanked Arnsparger profusely. And left the next day.

The Giants still talk about punter Joe Whelan, who came to camp as a free agent in 1968. Coach Allie Sherman took one look and cut him after the second day of practice. About ten days later, Sherman spotted Whelan eating in the cafeteria.

"What are you doing here?" Sherman asked. "I thought I cut you two weeks ago?"

Whelan looked up from his lunch. "Oh, you did. It's just that nobody told me I had to go home."

This is the time to get a leg up on the rest of your National Football League competitors. For borderline players, conditioning and hustling in training camp is the only way to make the roster. Free agents like Jim Burt and Brad Benson of the New York Giants made the team that way in their rookie seasons. Now, they're Pro Bowl players.

A TYPICAL TRAINING CAMP SCHEDULE

6:30–8:00	**Breakfast and physical therapy; taping**
8:00–8:30	**Offense and defense meetings**
8:30–9:00	**Special teams meeting**
8:50	**Specialists leave meetings**
9:00	**Specialists on field**
9:15–11:15	**Field practice**
11:45–12:30	**Lunch**
12:35	**Report for treatment**
12:35–1:15	**Taping for rookies**
12:35–2:15	**Rest**
2:15–2:55	**Taping for veterans**
3:00–4:00	**Offense and defense meetings**
4:00–4:15	**Specialists on field**
4:15–6:15	**Field practice**
6:45–7:30	**Dinner**
7:30	**Report for treatment**
8:00	**Evening offense and defense meetings and sometimes whole team talk**
11:00	**Bed**

The mode is different, but the message is the same. Football fans, after all, are football fans. Some Giants' fans (right) will go to any lengths to show their true colors—in this case, blue and red. Below, the New England Patriots' fans do have a way with words.

The Fan

The true football fan is everything the word implies: unreasonably enthusiastic, overly zealous. The fan is an emotional lightning rod; he rises and falls with the tide of the game.

For him, the highs are intense after victory and the lows…well, if he's a Giants' fan, he'd sooner hand over his firstborn than lose to the Washington Redskins. A tough loss on Sunday can make Monday even worse than it already is. A big loss can ruin the whole week and, in some cases, an entire off-season. The sensitive quarterback's feelings are hurt when he hears the boos, but when the fan pays his $20 he's entitled to scream anything that comes to mind. Of course, parental guidance is suggested out at the ballpark.

They are a pretty amazing group, on the whole. The Wave, that rising crest of humanity that sweeps around stadiums, is now the fan's signature. Creative it is not, but enthusiasm has never translated well into style. Look around a stadium on game day and see the spectrum of life itself. Here is a family of yuppies. Dad, a button-down study in khaki and loafers, leads the kids through some

Football's hold on the general population knows no demographical bounds. Fair (and foul) weather friends learn the game at the feet of their fathers, and before long they have the strength and convictions that result in felled goalposts.

OME
ACK HOME
TEVE + LYNN

The 1930's spawned pom-poms, and now, fifty years later, painted faces are the rage. (Below) Witness supporters of Kansas City Chiefs' quarterback Todd Blackledge, who are truly a two-faced breed. Others (right) also dress for excess. They include fans of the New York Giants, the Washington Redskins' offensive linemen (more commonly known as The Hogs), and any team that will let a gorilla in the stadium.

pretty complicated cheers. Earlier, the tailgate buffet included rack of lamb and a frivolous little Cabernet Sauvignon. There, on the other hand, is the hardcore fan and his college buddies. They seem to have taken their shirts off for some reason, which is a little strange because it's 20° F and the wind picks up with every passing play. "Antifreeze," says one of them, reaching to pick up a Big Beer. "We owe it all to antifreeze."

There are gorillas, furry orange creatures of questionable heritage, people with their faces painted any number of hues. There are little old ladies who have been coming to the game for twenty years and first-time thrill-seekers who knew somebody in the front office.

The signs are interesting, too, and are much more attractive than graffiti, and invariably more clever. WILL YOU MARRY ME, SUZI? ONLY IF THE PACKERS WIN!

And so on. Real fans wear the uniforms of their heroes to the game. The unbalanced fans wear them to bed. They dress in green from head to toe. Or orange. Or blue. Or red. They pay a great price to be here, even if they weren't forced to obtain their tickets through a scalper. They could be raking leaves or enjoying their families, but this is their choice for a crisp autumn Sunday.

That is what being a *fan*atic is all about.

Off The Field

There is a Catch-22 in professional football. A player works hard all his life to be recognized. Then, when he's finally made it to the top, he does anything short of an end-around to avoid the constant, nagging media attention. Dallas Cowboy Herschel Walker, however, is an exception to that rule. He happens to be one of the most genial, cooperative athletes in sport.

Football players are people, too. Which is to say, there are as many lifestyles as there are players. The wild ones—"Hollywood" Henderson, Lyle Alzado, Lawrence Taylor, and Jim McMahon—become legends.

"I play the game wild, and I live my life off the field the same way," says the Giants' Taylor, who may be the best football player ever to pull on shoulder pads. The greatest play of Taylor's life, however—on or off the field—was Kamikaze Night at a local bar during training camp one season. Amid much applause, Taylor stood on the

bar and threw himself toward the floor. He landed on his hands and pressed up into a handstand. The place exploded. Thus, are legends born.

Joe Paterno, the great coach at Penn State once said of his own methods, "We try to remember football is part of life—not life itself." That may work for scrubbed undergraduates, but where does the professional draw the line? When does he turn off the switch? Can he, even if he wants to?

Listen to the football player as he meets the press after the game. His answers are stac-

Lyle Alzado is a teddy bear. Really. His agent—the one who gets him all those terrific television commercials for dandruff shampoo—says so. Why then do you get the distinct impression that Alzado is reacting to some on-field disaster with a trace of glee? This is one teddy bear who spit-shined his opponents for years as a Raider.

cato bursts, followed by long silences. Blood, sweat, and tears for all to see. Emotions race around a locker room at a frantic rate. And that's not necessarily all. Controlled substances have been known to find their way into some players' systems.

It's all part of the game.

And when the clock runs out, the motor is still running. Drinks invariably are on the house, so celebrate, my man.

More than any other player, Bobby Layne epitomized the larger-than-life football player. The Hall of Fame quarterback would invariably lead his teammates to a nearby bar after another dreary practice at old Tiger Stadium. He was a regular nighthawk whose system not only thrived on reveling, but seemed to demand it.

Layne played from 1948 to 1962 and led the Lions to three NFL championships in that time. His was also one of the first big names to be associated with the gaming tables of Las Vegas. In sum, Layne represented everything today's NFL abhors.

Gambling remains the greatest fear. Experts estimate that Americans bet more than $1 billion annually on football games. This, in itself, doesn't seem to bother the football people as much as it does the U.S. government, which is missing out on all that taxable income. Even the most staid newspaper provides fans with point spreads of upcoming games.

It is the very appearance of wrongdoing that threatens the league's integrity, however. That is why Paul Hornung of the Green Bay Packers and Detroit's Alex Karras were suspended for one season by Commissioner Pete Rozelle in 1963. The evidence was never overwhelming, but it didn't matter much.

Joe Willie Namath was another player known to like a good time. He drove fast cars and was seen with beautiful women. (Or was that the other way around?) The New York Jets quarterback wore white shoes on the football field and sported a Fu Manchu mustache at a time when personal rebellion was in vogue. He was the sports world's anti-hero in an era of anti-heros. He even *guaranteed* a Super Bowl III victory against the Baltimore Colts—and then delivered. It is said that the

It takes all kinds to play the game of football. Chicago Bears' quarterback Jim McMahon (left) has always been an outrageous character. Hollywood Henderson (right) dressed as flashily as he played for the Dallas Cowboys. (Below) Chicago guard Tom Thayer (No. 57) and Atlanta guard John Scully typify the burly men of the trenches.

Jets' shocking 16–7 win cemented the merger between the NFL and the old AFL. And it was all the result of the sheer force of Namath's personality.

Solid citizens are what the NFL wants. Isn't it interesting, therefore, that the rebels are the ones fans take to their hearts? Take McMahon, a latter-day Namath or Layne. Before Super Bowl XX was over, the Chicago Bears' quarterback had offended his opponents, the women of New Orleans, and even his coach. At Pat O'Brien's, the famed watering hole near Bourbon Street, McMahon and his teammates were seen four days before the game. They came twenty-nine strong and

stayed for hours. And hours. There was McMahon, a happily married man, bouncing a blonde on each knee. Hurricanes—those flammable red concoctions—flowed freely and so did the Bears the followir. Sunday—all over the New England Patriots.

Outrageousness? Well, yes. And the general public couldn't seem to get enough. Six books came out of that super 1985–1986 season. And the biggest story, quite literally, was "The Fridge." Just an average 300-pound rookie nose tackle until Chicago coach Mike Ditka gave him the ball, soon William Perry was blocking, running for touchdowns, and trying to carry Walter Payton into the end zone. Perry became a phenomenon, a gargantuan Everyman, if such a thing is possible.

The fast-food people came running—couldn't Perry eat twenty-six Big Macs at one sitting? The soda people weren't far behind—didn't he wash those hamburgers down with seven gallons of Coke? If it could be endorsed, Perry's name was on it or behind it. During the 1986 season, America's school children voted Perry their favorite professional athlete. It was the pinnacle, because The Fridge never recaptured that magic. As one veteran of the league told him at the height of his popularity, "Put it in the bank while you can."

The smart football players become part of the scenery after their playing days. Sometimes, their field personalities, if properly cultivated, flourish beyond the white lines. Alzado, the former Raiders defensive end, doesn't spit on opponents anymore, but he plays tough for the camera as he washes away potential dandruff in the shower. Dick Butkus, maybe the meanest, nastiest linebacker to ever play the game, smiles a cuddly smile and sells a sporting magazine. Roger Staubach, the old Dallas Cowboys quarterback, pushes life insurance, among other things.

Staubach is one of football's good guys. Make no mistake, they're out there. It's just that they don't make good copy. See Giants nose tackle Jim Burt snuggling with Jim Burt, Jr. It's not exactly front-page news.

That's why the world needs more football players like Jim McMahon. He represents all that is good—and bad—about the game. As Layne becomes Namath, and Namath becomes McMahon, it is reassuring to know that the chain remains unbroken.

Athletes are people, too. Yet, sometimes it's easy to forget that when they're inside helmets and under all those pads. John Riggins (left) the former Washington Redskins' fullback, always marched to a different drummer. He arrived at training camp one year with an impressive Mohican haircut. (Below) Giants' nose tackle, Jim Burt, a pussycat with his son, was a madman in college, according to his Miami roommates.

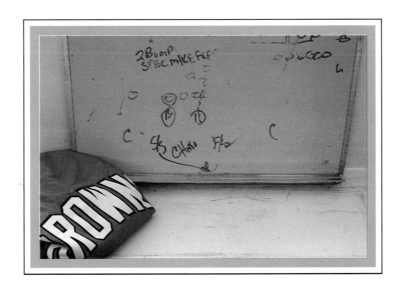

See New York Jets' quarterback, Richard Todd, fade back to pass. See him fade completely as Miami's Kim Bokamper arrives ominously from behind. Hear the hot breath of Green Bay Packers' defensive end, Robert Brown(below),coming closer and closer to Giants' quarterback Phil Simms. Hear the curse of the offensive lineman who just let Brown slip by. See Simms crumple in a tiny heap.

Blitzes and Sacks

Most of the time, the offense dictates circumstances on a football field. Action, followed by reaction on the part of the defense. Most of the time.

The blitz can be the great equalizer. It is how the defense strikes back, the startling means by which the defenders take the offensive and the offenders become overly defensive. To have your quarterback knocked on his behind, or mauled in some other fashion, is an embarrassment of the highest order.

Rushing the passer is a formalized part of the game. That three or four defenders will test the offensive line on every play is to be expected. The blitz, however, operates on the premise of surprise. Most often, linebackers are the second line of defense behind the ends and the tackles. Usually, they make the tackles on running plays and drop into pass coverage. But every now and then, they sneak into the backfield. And when that happens, watch out.

We have all seen that horrible collision. The quarterback drops back in the

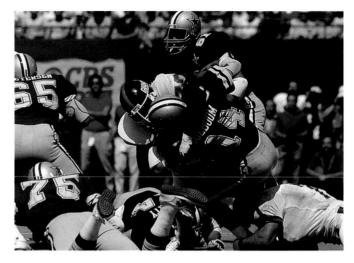

pocket to read the defensive secondary when—*zap!*—he is blind-sided by a streaking blur. The ball squirts free and the unfortunate blitzee lies on the ground, trying to force his breath past battered ribs.

Of course, the blitz blows up in the defense's face just as often as it succeeds. If the appointed executioner betrays his blitz in any way, the quarterback is trained to throw the ball to the vacated spot. That usually means trouble. In such a situation, it becomes a race against time. Can the quarterback release the ball before the blitz reaches him?

It is on such all-or-nothing questions that professional football revolves on.

(Above) The sack unfolds. New York Giants' defensive end, Leonard Marshall (No. 70) has broken past a Dallas Cowboys' offensive lineman who shall remain nameless, and quarterback Gary Hogeboom slowly, sadly falls back to earth. (Left) Philadelphia Eagles' quarterback, Ron Jaworski, is wrapped up by longtime nemesis, Lawrence Taylor, the ethereal linebacker for the New York Giants. Sacks are not pretty.

(Left) The New York Jets'
quarterback gets a pass off
against Richard Bishop of
the New England Patriots.
The question is, though,
will he live to tell about it?

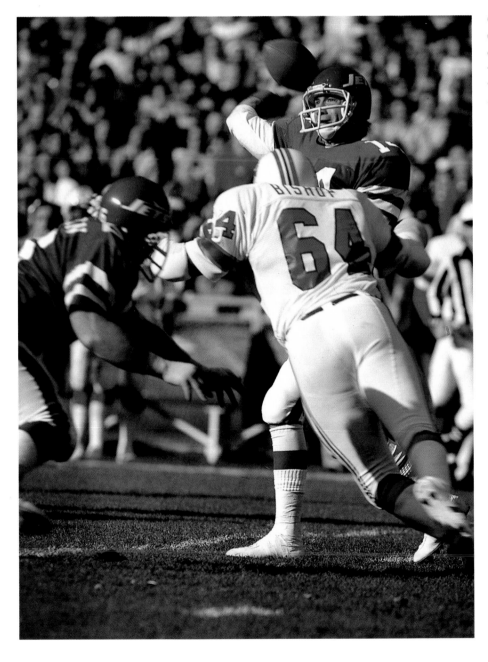

The Sweep

This is what football is about. Our guys. Your guys. Let's rumble; let's see who's better.

Call it what you will. Vince Lombardi's old Green Bay Packers used to run the power sweep so much they should have patented it. The University of Southern California has a catchier name—Student Body Left or Student Body Right, depending on which side of the field they want to rumble. In a game that has seen sweeping changes, the sweep has remained the same. And it has always been the basic test of strength between offense and defense.

In the crucible of the trenches, might always makes right. There are no play-action passes, no fakes, no deception of any kind. Just hand the ball to the running back and watch the play develop.

Here comes the tight end, leading the play and taking out the opposing outside linebacker. There's the tackle looking to pin the defensive end. The guards make it all happen. Ordinarily, they muck around the line of scrimmage with a lot of finesse. But here's where they earn their money. They loop toward the point of attack, gathering themselves for a meeting with destiny— and an inside linebacker. It's not often you see a 270-pound man so earnest in his frenzy.

The running back has several options. If the play works as designed, he will bounce outside, turn the corner, and—hopefully—move a good way down the sideline. Sometimes, the defensive end has a mind of his own. Then the play gets turned inside, or stopped completely.

Every team has this play in its repertoire It's the really good ones that make it work.

Here it is: the textbook sweep. (Left) Ken O'Brien of the New York Jets pitches the ball to halfback Johnny Hector. A sweep goes according to plan (right) when Freeman NcNeil breaks around a tackle and into the end zone. (Below) Philadelphia quarterback, Ron Jaworski, prepares to deliver for a play to the right.

The Bomb

Chicago Bear Doug Flutie (above) shown here when he used to play for the now-defunct New Jersey Generals of the United States Football League, may have thrown the most famous bomb of all time while still a quarterback for Boston College. When he launched the Hail Flutie pass to beat Miami in the waning moments of the Orange Bowl, Flutie guaranteed himself, in a six-second span, a lifetime of riches. Not bad for one pass. Tony Eason (right) of the New England Patriots is another modern day Mad Bomber.

Check the dictionary. Next to the word *hubris* is a tiny picture of Joe Namath or Daryle Lamonica reaching back and throwing the football as far as they can.

The bomb. Has sort of a subtle ring to it, doesn't it? If executed properly, it can truly wreck havoc and destruction.

In this time of ball control and three-yard swing passes to the fullback, the bomb doesn't have the attraction it once did. Certainly, getting your touchdowns with slow, grinding drives keeps the defense off the field longer. But there is nothing quite as demoralizing as having some strong-armed farm boy flinging a pass sixty yards in the air over the entire defense and into the hands of a fleet wide receiver for a touchdown.

Today's bend-but-don't-break prevent defenses do not allow it to happen often. Most teams assign a safety to handle any deep traffic. Still, there are times when that wideout only has one man to beat. And that is when the cocky quarterback smiles to himself at the line of scrimmage and tries not to drool.

Unlike a typical running play or mid-range pass, there is no margin for error here. The ball and the receiver just arrive at precisely the same point in time. It doesn't happen often because this is the game's most difficult play to execute properly. But unlike most get-rich-quick schemes, this one usually pays instant dividends.

If not? Incomplete pass. Nothing ventured, nothing gained. The quarterback can always fling it again.

If everyone along the offensive line does his job properly, if the quarterback throws the ball deftly enough, if the receiver breaks free and runs down the ball, there is a chance for a big play. That's why they call it a home run.

The ball is already in the air and every eye in the nervous stadium follows it to its natural conclusion. The wide receiver, for whom the ball is intended, leaps high with the opposing defensive back. Just because it has been thrown to him doesn't mean the wideout has any claim on the ball. The politics of football show no favoritism. He who is swifter and jumps higher wins the ball.

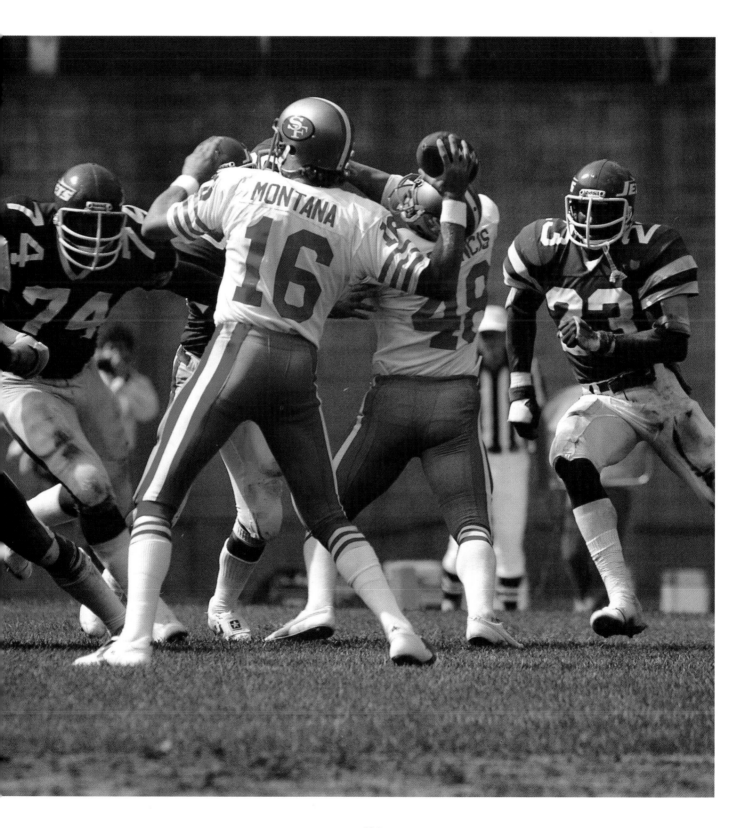

The New York Jets' Mark Gastineau (note the proud stance) has just broken through the Kansas City Chiefs' offensive line and leveled quarterback Todd Blackledge. Ouch. This is the kind of play where momentum begins and ends.

The Big Hit

Once a game, sometimes twice, there is a breathtaking moment when two desperately careening bodies meet and one of them goes backward. It is sudden impact of an entirely different kind.

"That shot in the second quarter really got us down," the losing coach says after the game. "He got his bell rung. It really took the wind out of our sails."

Football players are people, too, after all. They are not blind. When one of their own gets clocked and leaves the field on a stretcher or heads for the wrong sideline, they take notice.

The greatest hits are grim reminders of the mayhem all that speed and size can produce. That's what the victim is thinking, if he can think anything at all just then. The guy who dished it out, though, can't wipe the smile off his face.

ZAP! ZOWIE! CRUNCH! That's the sound of New York Jets' running back Freeman McNeil (left) getting drilled by a host of Houston Oilers—and they say football players are overpaid. Dallas Cowboys running back Tony Dorsett (above) reaches for a deep breath after a tackle of Giant proportions.

(Above) The quarterback, lying shattered in the fetal position, is always the target of zealous defensive lineman. In this case it's Jets' Mark Gastineau who did the damage.

Touchdown!

"…Smith takes the snap, he hands the ball to Jones, who rips off right tackle. He avoids the tackler at the three, he cuts left, he…

Touchdown!!!"

In football, it doesn't get any better than this. Do it enough times and you'll win every week. This is why they play—to score six points and bring a stadium to its collective feet. This is why teams spend the off-season watching old game films, why they go through the grim formality of training camp.

Never mind the fans and the officials. Watch the players on the field and you'll know who just penetrated the heart of enemy territory. The slump-ing bodies belong to the vanquished. Those guys frolicking in the end zone just got a shot of adrenaline.

It used to be that a good old-fashioned spike of the football was the appropriate exclamation point at the end of successful scoring play. But in recent years individual expression has replaced the spike. Billy "White Shoes" Johnson started it all with a special sort of dance that involved sensational knee control. Washington's "Fun Bunch" had a terrific five-man high-five number that brought choreography to football. By 1985, the celebratory antics of the "Me Generation" had grown so sophisticated the

If the bottom line is scoring, then nothing tops the feeling of a touchdown. Freeman NcNeil (above) of the New York Jets coasts into the end zone ahead of a Cincinnati defender. Even a photographer cannot resist celebrating.

In case you missed it, in case the thunder of the crowd diverted your attention, in case the wild player celebration passed you by...the officials are there to confirm the undeniable truth—Touchdown!

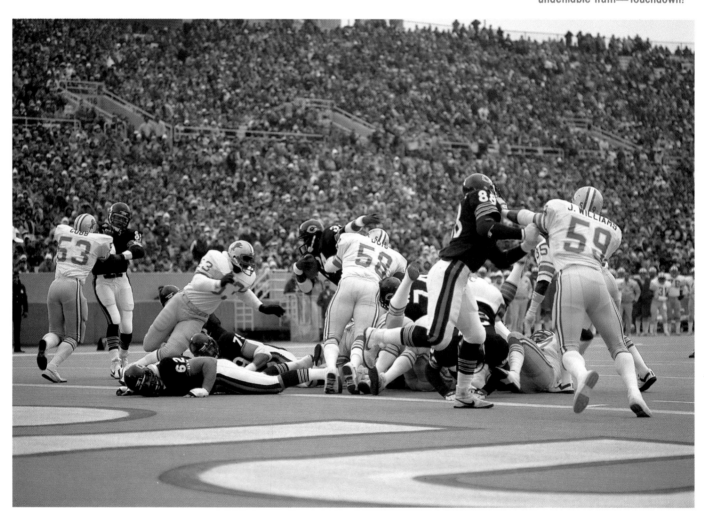

Walter Payton of the Chicago Bears (behind No. 58) is about to split two Detroit Lions' linebackers on his way to the end zone. When he does, it's a safe bet Soldier Field will go fairly crazy.

National Football League felt it necessary to pass a silly law prohibiting non-spontaneous combustion after a particularly big play. It was aimed in particular at New York Jets defensive end Mark Gastineau, who liked to sack-dance after leveling opposing quarterbacks. Nevertheless, it effectively muted all scoring celebrations.

These days, officials don't like to throw the flag when the celebrating starts. Scoring, after all, is a part of the game. Celebrating those good times is important, too.

The star-spangled bottom line at the Super Bowl: bigger is better. Biggest, naturally, is best. The anticipation is everything. See the crowd milling around the Rose Bowl at Pasadena before the game. Sense the excitement the game never seems to live up to.

Being There

The name says it all.

Football's best heads got together before the 1966 season desperately seeking an identity for their newest creation. The champions of the American Football League and the National Football League would clash in one glorious contest at season's end. Such an idea! Now, what to call it?

The American-National Football World Championship? Too long. The Game? Harvard and Yale had the patent on it. The Astro Bluebonnet Bowl? Already taken, believe it or not. The Mega Bowl? Not bad. The Ultimate Bowl? Well, almost.

Thus, the Super Bowl was born. It was a terrific handle, taking in all the hyperbole and glitz and silliness that the event has come to represent. But there was hardly anything super about the first few games. Vince Lombardi's Green Bay Packers wasted the Kansas City Chiefs 35-10 in 1967's Super Bowl I before only 61,946 at Memorial Coliseum in Los Angeles. Then the Packers ripped up the Oakland Raiders, 33-14, a year later. This was some fun, wasn't it?

And then quarterback Joe Namath and the New York Jets changed everything. They came into Super Bowl III as seventeen-point underdogs to the Baltimore Colts, the NFL's fat cats. Oh sure, Namath predicted a victory, but he was just talking through the hat on his swelled head. Or was he?

The Jets, true to Namath's word, shocked, the Colts 16-7 and the Super Bowl was on its way to becoming superb. The Jets victory virtually forced a merger between the leagues.

And so, each January the champions of the American Football Conference and the National Football Conference meet in a game that never seems to live up to its name. That, however, is not the point. No, the point is the rich color and pageantry surrounding the event. Or something like that…

First of all, there is the big build up. For sixteen weeks, football teams play every Sunday or Monday. Then there is a grand pause for the Super Bowl. For the first week the annointed ones catch their breath; then comes seven disjointed days under a media microscope. The coaches work up the game plan and, if they're smart, get the delicate game preparation under their team's belt before the media blitz.

There is nothing quite like it in sport. *Much Ado About Nothing* could have been The Bard's vision of the Super Bowl future, for the smallest, most trivial details are fodder for the more than 3,000 accredited media types, all hacking around for a different angle. Does the star quarterback have a cold? Is he taking proper medication? Will a stuffy nose break his concentration in the huddle? Will his teammates respect his raspy play-calling? Does anyone care? The big story as the Super Bowl celebrated its twentieth anniversary was the accupuncturist of Chicago quarterback Jim McMahon. During Super Bowl week, a few pins and needles in a particular Bears' behind can

approach the gravity of world hunger or terrorism in the Mid-East.

Football players have always been a little on the wild side, but it is a revelation every year when a group of defensive linemen take New Orleans or Pasadena or Tampa by storm. A few beers can turn into a flood of barley and hops. A scuffle becomes a conflagration. "Mayhem in the A.M." shrieks one New York City tabloid. You get the idea.

Super Bowls are about adulation. The long-suffering fan finally gets his wish: the team is in the Big One. He gets the week off from work, scrambles for airline tickets—forget about Super Bowl tickets for now. Upon landing, he buys all the football souvenirs and regalia he can lay his hands on. Then, off to the hotel for some serious lobby-watching. Here's Joe Morris, there's Harry Carson. Look, Jerome Sally. He's only the third string nose tackle, but he'll make a marvelous picture here by the potted fern. Autographs—on pennants, hats, arms, and unmentionable areas—are sought. Field position, as it pertains to the busy hotel lobby, takes on a whole new meaning.

Drinks are mandatory.

Whether Denver Broncos' fans were willing to admit it or not, their team was a heavy underdog in Super Bowl XXI. The Giants tried to say nice things all week long about their worthy opponents, but they knew they were going to win. They knew. Led by linebacker Gary Reasons, (foreground) the Giants donned their capes the day before the Super Bowl in front of the Rose Bowl. The next day, they played like supermen.

They're the lubrication that makes the whole thing work. You cannot turn around without someone offering a little something. Hospitality, thy name is Super Bowl. As a result, everyone is a little more docile—to a point. Then belligerence sets in and things get ugly. Fans wearing jackets with conflicting mascots have been known to rumble. Some of these flaps rival the action that ultimately takes place on the field.

Those are the commoners. The beautiful people are off in a forty-five-foot Chris Craft, taking in the trés-trendy California view at Newport Beach Harbor. A crew of three guys who sound Swedish— they're wearing turquoise cummerbunds—keep all the guests happy as clams. This is a happening party, all right. Good Lord, the party favors are human.

These outbursts occur all weekend long, right up until kickoff. The monster gala is a Friday night affair in which football celebrates itself in fairly berserk fashion. It really is quite an effort. The scene is always a cavernous convention hall, or a city of massive

Although the men on the field engage in battle, the fans play nice at the Super Bowl. Note the lone Broncos' fan in the sea of Giants supporters to the right. See what a few beers and a couple of T-shirts can do for your spirits?

tents. There is the requisite theme, say, "Hooray for Hollywood." Humphrey Bogart, Charlie Chaplin, and Clark Gable doubles mingle with the masses—and they don't begin to compete with the real people there. An Italian film crew actually shoots footage of the guests. There are stages everywhere with dancers, singers, jugglers and the like. The food borders on the ridiculous; the vegetables, garnished cleverly, are heaped in piles big enough to irrigate. The iced shrimp, Florida stone crabs, and oysters on the halfshell are imposing. Consider the barbequed turkey, the steak tartar, the honey-baked ribs, if you will. Now, how about a delightful raspberry sorbet for dessert? And some white wine all around.

After eating, Captain Cardiac and the Coronaries bop out hits of the '50s. Bruce Willis takes a turn at the microphone and wails "Roll Over Beethoven." The place erupts. Later, much later, the carnival all begins to blur.

This is the essence of the Super Bowl. And then on Sunday they play a football game.

Before the big game, it's easy to tell who has tickets and who does not. The former can be found partying with friends and strangers alike; the latter resort to clever signs and outright bribes in a last minute attempt to see the game.

Phil Simms became one of only eight quarterbacks to win the Most Valuable Player in twenty-one Super Bowls, completing twenty-two of twenty-five passes. Simms was very nearly perfect against the Broncos.

SUPER BOWL MOST VALUABLE PLAYER AWARDS

I	**Bart Starr**, Quarterback, Green Bay
II	**Bart Starr**, Quarterback, Green Bay
III	**Joe Namath**, Quarterback, N.Y. Jets
IV	**Len Dawson**, Quarterback, Kansas City
V	**Chuck Howley**, Linebacker, Dallas
VI	**Roger Staubach**, Quarterback, Dallas
VII	**Jake Scott**, Safety, Miami
VIII	**Larry Csonka**, Running Back, Miami
IX	**Franco Harris**, Running Back, Pittsburgh
X	**Lynn Swann**, Wide Receiver, Pittsburgh
XI	**Fred Biletnikoff**, Wide Receiver, Oakland
XII	**Harvey Martin**, Defensive End and **Randy White**, Defensive Tackle, Dallas
XIII	**Terry Bradshaw**, Quarterback, Pittsburgh
XIV	**Terry Bradshaw**, Quarterback, Pittsburgh
XV	**Jim Plunkett**, Quarterback, Oakland
XVI	**Joe Montana**, Quarterback, San Francisco
XVII	**John Riggins**, Running Back, Washington
XVIII	**Marcus Allen**, Running Back, Los Angeles
XIX	**Joe Montana**, Quarterback, San Francisco
XX	**Richard Dent**, Defensive End, Chicago
XXI	**Phil Simms**, Quarterback, N.Y. Giants

SUPER BOWL TV RATINGS

		Rating
1.	XVI, San Francisco 26, Cincinnati 21, 1982 (CBS)	49.1
2.	XVII, Washington 27, Miami 17, 1983 (NBC)	48.6
3.	XX, Chicago 46, New England 10, 1986 (NBC)	48.3
4.	XXI, N.Y. Giants 39, Denver 20 (CBS)	47.8
5.	XII, Dallas 27, Denver 10, 1978 (CBS)	47.2
6.	XIII, Pittsburgh 35, Dallas 31, 1979 (NBC)	47.1
7.	XVIII, L.A. Raiders 38, Washington 9, 1984 (CBS)	46.4
7.	XIX, San Francisco 38, Miami 16, 1985 (ABC)	46.4
9.	XIV, Pittsburgh 31, L.A. Rams 19, 1980 (CBS)	46.3
10.	XI, Oakland 32, Minnesota 14, 1977 (NBC)	44.4
10.	XV, Oakland 27, Philadelphia 10, 1981 (NBC)	44.4
12.	VI, Dallas 24, Miami 3, 1972 (CBS)	44.2
13.	VII, Miami 14, Washington 7, 1973 (NBC)	42.7
14.	IX, Pittsburgh 16, Minnesota 6, 1975 (NBC)	42.4
15.	X, Pittsburgh 21, Dallas 17, 1976 (NBC)	42.3
16.	VIII, Miami 24, Minnesota 7, 1974 (CBS)	41.6
17.	V, Baltimore 16, Dallas 13, 1971 (NBC)	39.9
18.	IV, Kansas City 23, Minnesota 7, 1970 (CBS)	39.4
19.	II, Green Bay 33, Oakland 14, 1968 (CBS)	36.8
20.	III, N.Y. Jets 16, Baltimore 7, 1969 (NBC)	36.0
21.	I, Green Bay 35, Kansas City 10, 1967 (CBS)	23.0
	(NBC)	17.8

The numerical rating indicates the percentage of viewers at the time actually tuned in to the program.

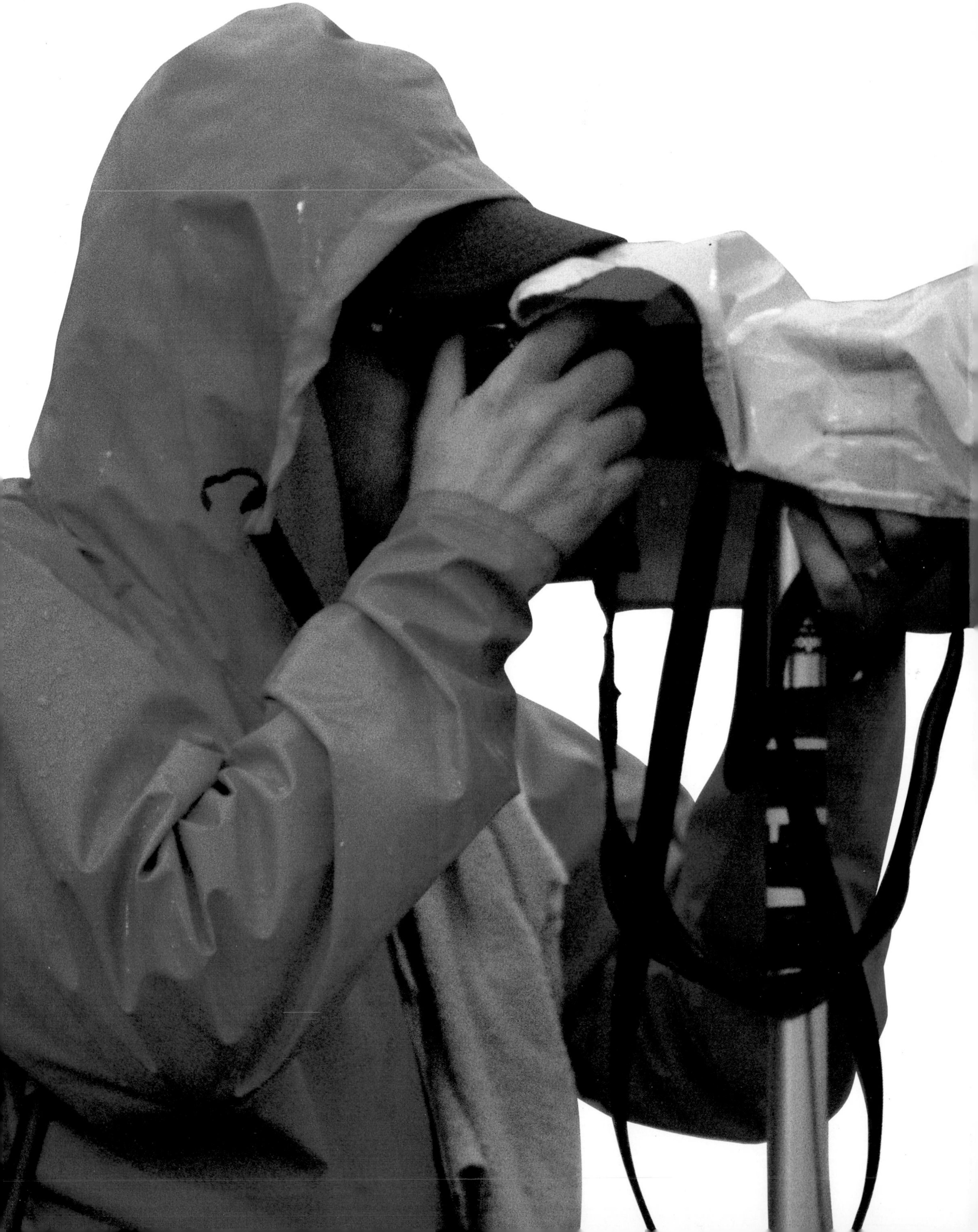

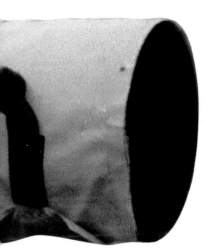

Nothing, absolutely nothing, escapes the long arm of the photographer. Inside that small television camera, millions of eyes from all over are watching.

SUPER BOWL WINNERS

I	Green Bay 35, Kansas City 10
II	Green Bay 33, Oakland 14
III	N.Y. Jets 16, Baltimore 7
IV	Kansas City 23, Minnesota 7
V	Baltimore 16, Dallas 13
VI	Dallas 24, Miami 3
VII	Miami 14, Washington 7
VIII	Miami 24, Minnesota 7
IX	Pittsburgh 16, Minnesota 6
X	Pittsburgh 21, Dallas 17
XI	Oakland 32, Minnesota 14
XII	Dallas 27, Denver 10
XIII	Pittsburgh 35, Dallas 31
XIV	Pittsburgh 31, Los Angeles 19
XV	Oakland 27, Philadelphia 10
XVI	San Francisco 26, Cincinnati 21
XVII	Washington 27, Miami 17
XVIII	Los Angeles 38, Washington 9
XIX	San Francisco 38, Miami 16
XX	Chicago 46, New England 10
XXI	N.Y. Giants 39, Denver 20